# Lost Travel Found

## Turning Pain into Purpose

Ashley Jackson

ISBN: 978-0-578-90520-4

# Dedication

Dad, this is for YOU! Thanks for all the laughter, conversations, and love! I carry your wisdom with me each day on my life's journey. I am my Father's daughter!

Troy, my Prince Charming, and love. I never knew there was a love like this before. Through our journey, I have learned things about myself and you and the amount of strength that we have may be unparalleled. I love us and I love you. Forever. No matter where life's path takes us, I know we will navigate it together.

Mom, My Queen, and my best friend. I couldn't have gotten through life without you! You are my rock and continue to pick me up when I fall. You deserve the world! I love you.

# Contents

**Foreword** ..............................................................**vii**

**Acknowledgement** ..............................................**xi**

**Intro** .......................................................................**1**

**Section 1: Lost** ....................................................**3**

Chapter 1: "Good Times" ....................................5

Chapter 2: "Thriller" .............................................9

Chapter 3: "Don't Stop Believin'" .................... 13

Chapter 4: "Endless Love" ............................... 15

Chapter 5: "Party Up" ....................................... 19

Chapter 6: "Eye Of The Tiger" ......................... 25

Chapter 7: "Address To The Stars" ................. 29

Chapter 8: "Why Don't We Fall in Love" ......... 31

Chapter 9: "Hero" .............................................. 35

Chapter 10: "Can't Feel My Face" ................... 37

Chapter 11: "God's Not Done With You" ......... 39

Chapter 12: "Runaway" ..................................... 43

**Section 2: Travel** ..............................................**49**

Chapter 13: "One Love" .................................... 51

Chapter 14: "Leaving On A Jet Plane" ............. 53

Chapter 15 - "Lean On Me" ............................... 61

Chapter 16: "Best Friend" ................................. 65

Chapter 17: "Brown Skin Girl" .......................... 73

Chapter 18: "Miss You Much" ........................... 81

Chapter 19: "Scream" ....................................... 89

Chapter 20: "Remember The Time" .................. 99

Chapter 21: "Soon As I Get Home" ............................107

Chapter 22: "This Will Be" ............................109

Chapter 23: "Can You Stand The Rain" ............................113

**Section 3: Found** ............................ **117**

Chapter 24: "Can't Give Up Now" ............................119

Chapter 25: "Looking For You" ............................121

Chapter 26: "It Will All Be Worth It" ............................129

Chapter 27: "Fear" ............................147

Chapter 28: "When You Believe" ............................151

Chapter 29: "Superwoman" ............................161

Chapter 30: "Count On Me" ............................165

Chapter 31: "Until The End Of Time" ............................169

Chapter 32: "Dance With My Father" ............................173

Chapter 33: "The Doctor Said" ............................175

Chapter 34: "Always And Forever" ............................179

Chapter 35: "Your Joy" ............................185

Chapter 36: "Weathered" ............................189

Chapter 37: "The Champion" ............................195

Chapter 38: "Love You More" ............................197

Chapter 39: "Girl On Fire" ............................201

Chapter 40: "Superstar" ............................207

Chapter 41: "You'll Be In My Heart" ............................209

Chapter 42: "When You Wish Upon A Star" ............................211

**References** ............................ **215**

**Resources** ............................ **219**

# Foreword

I help women overcome limiting thoughts and sabotaging behaviors and discover and monetize their purpose and passions so they can experience more joy, wealth, freedom, and impact. I'm who you call when you know you're not living the life you want to live nor doing the work you want to do. When you know God has a higher calling on your life. When you know you want to live a life of service to others so you can make a difference in the world. But you don't know what to do or where to start to try to fill the emptiness and restlessness in your soul. That was the foundation for my first phone conversation with Ashley Jackson.

She had started following me on social media due to our shared passion for travel and my freedom-based business which allowed me to work from anywhere in the world. But it was the past few, less-than-joyous chapters of Ashley's life that had led her to schedule a fateful, life-changing coaching call with me.

Ashley was the epitome of what I see with so many women. As natural givers and nurturers, we often give and nurture at the expense of our own self. We put ourselves on the back burner of our own lives even as we uplift, support, and care for everyone else. Our identity becomes defined by the people we love and their needs and desires. And what happens is that we lose little pieces of ourselves over time, until one day, we look in the mirror and we don't even recognize the woman looking back at us. We don't know who we are or what happened to the woman we used to be. That was the Ashley I first spoke to.

She had been on an emotional roller-coaster for the past few years. A long, exhausting, almost overwhelming journey of epic highs and lows, the likes of which few people will ever experience. A jaw-dropping journey that put the role of *"caregiver"* and the vows of *"in sickness and in health"* to the test, in a way few people can even fathom.

But through that multi-faceted ordeal, Ashley learned patience, empathy, and grace and found courage and strength she never knew she had. She reached a place few people do... where we consciously and literally savor and celebrate the smallest details of life that we often taken for granted, such as opening our eyes in the morning or drawing our next breath. She found her life's purpose and the tribe of God-assigned people that she had been uniquely equipped to serve. Not just because of her gifts, skills, and talents. Not just because of her bubbly personality, ever-ready smile, or sensitive and compassionate nature. But because of how she weathered the most painful period of her life and the valuable lessons she learned while navigating it. And last, but certainly not least, I believe Ashley knows better than most what love, commitment, and selflessness truly look like in a marriage.

So, Ashley, on behalf of everyone (because we all experience dark days and need a beacon of light to show us the way), I want to thank you for being a tangible example of the mythological Phoenix. You emerged from the ashes of grief, despair, and heartache with new-found purpose, passion, resilience, and determination. Your inspiring story reminds us of the power and resolve of the human spirit and will. It strengthens our faith and gives us hope and affirms that of the three things that last forever – faith, hope, and love – the greatest of these truly is love. It proves that pain can be redeemed and that all things – good and bad – can come together for our greater good. And it confirms that God, not man, always has the final say-so!

Sonjia "Lioness" Mackey
Owner and CEO, (Im)Possible Living, LLC

*"Nothing is impossible, the word itself says 'I'm possible'!"*

*– Audrey Hepburn*

# Acknowledgement

Paul, my brother, and best man. I know life hasn't always been nice or easy to us, but we have grown stronger together. You know I will always have your back. I often catch myself staring at you, because of how much you look like Dad. Walk out his legacy, my brother. I love you.

To both of my grandparents, Nana and Grandpa...I love you! You both have shown unwavering support for me, whether it was my crazy travel adventures or new business ventures, you are always there. You both have shown me what it means to be strong in this world, a world that continues to throw you curveballs. Because of you both, I can be!

My newfound sister, Meriam. I thank you for helping me stay accountable to my own boldness and identity. The divine brought us together to walk this path and work on our mission together, so that ALL caregivers can and will be heard! May God bless your steps.

Sonjia "Lioness" Mackey, business coach extraordinaire! You helped the Phoenix within rise above the ashes and take this world by storm! I will forever remember your coaching sessions and I will continue to share my passions and purpose with the world! Thank you for your commitment to my story.

To all the friends and family members that I mentioned

in the book or didn't get a chance to mention, I thank you! You all prayed for me, prayed for our family, and prayed for Troy when we needed it most. God bless you all!

# *Intro*

*"It has been said, 'time heals all wounds'. I do not agree. The wounds remain. In time, the mind, protecting its sanity, covers them with scar tissue and the pain lessens, but it is never gone."*

*- Rose Kennedy.*

My scar tissue is the pain and hurt I carry with me from my Dad's untimely death.

My scar tissue is the reluctance to have children due to my Dad's untimely death and fear of Troy's future health.

My scar tissue is knowing that even though Troy's doctors had a hand in his healing, the medical industry is still a business, and not everyone has the chance to receive the proper care they deserve.

My scar tissue is the many days/nights of self-reflection I had to do. Can I be strong enough for Troy? Can I really pull this wedding off and carry the burden of being a caregiver at the same time?

My scar tissue is watching my friends and family live carefree lives, while sometimes I feel like I'm in prison.

# SECTION 1:
## Lost

# CHAPTER 1:

## "Good Times"

### -Chic

W hen my Dad would ask, "Who wants to go for a ride?" I knew that good music, a deep discussion, and most likely a delicious bucket of chicken from Chicken Louie's was going to happen. Chicken Louie's had the BEST fried chicken in Dayton, OH; it was finger-licking good! It was always special to make that drive with him and get that delicious chicken, hearing the same stories repeatedly, but with each telling, they got more dramatic and funnier! I feel like therefore I have such an old soul...Al Green, The O'Jays, Kool & the Gang, Chic, Sister Sledge, and The Ohio Players would be blasting from his Jeep speakers. He would talk about the times that he went out to the club (before he met Mom) and would be grooving on the floor. The way my Dad described himself, he OWNED that floor! I pictured this tall, well-dressed, good-looking black man walk in and point at the DJ, and the DJ would instantly play Sister Sledge's: "He's the Greatest Dancer", and he would boogie on down!

Some of my favorite songs to listen to in those car rides

were Chic's "I Want Your Love" and "Freak Out", also Kool and the Gang's "Celebration", "Fresh", and "Hollywood Swinging". It is so interesting to hear how the musicians from my parents' era influenced the present-day music we hear on the radio now! I remember my Dad always saying that this is "real" singing and what we listen to on the radio was garbage. I used to disagree with him, but now that I am older...he was right! Imagine how that works!

I specifically remember one car ride when he told me that this one was just for us! I was so excited, me being a huge Daddy's girl, I was going to get him all to myself! I was about 13 or 14 at that time, and he wanted to talk to me about boys and how he knew I was growing up. At first, I was mortified because I didn't want to talk about this with my Dad, but I knew we needed to have this conversation. My Dad talked to me about how in the future when someone wanted to date me, how they should approach me and then HIM. I kept rolling my eyes, but deep down, I knew he was right. My Dad and Mom raised me to be strong and independent, but the inevitable would eventually happen...one day, I would like a boy, and he would like me back! It was important for me to understand how I should be treated and talked to, so if some boy came around and was less than, I knew to keep it moving.

You would think with me being so equipped with all this knowledge, that I wouldn't have made mistakes when it came to matters of the heart...right? HA! I made plenty of mistakes or learning curves, as I like to lovingly put it now. With each heartbreak, I almost felt like I was letting my parents down as well. Of course, they never said that or did anything for me to come to that conclusion, but that is how my mind worked then. The one guy that my Dad didn't get to meet, the one guy who loves all of me, the one guy who swept me off my feet, the one guy who took me to Cinderella's castle and proposed, the one guy who I went through hell and back with--would be the one that was the most WORTHY of my Dad's blessing, and the one that treated me how my Dad told me I ought to be treated. Funny how life works.

# CHAPTER 2:

## *"Thriller"*

-Michael Jackson

PURPOSE DRIVEN, DREAM CHASER...no words have been spoken or written to describe who my father is! My Dad is a great man of character and morals who loved both his family and church family to pieces; he also is a "big picture" thinker; he never allowed his surroundings to suppress his dreams. My Dad, Paul "Skip" Jackson, is a tall man (he was an incredible basketball player in his day) with a big vision, loud laugh, and loving heart. Dad instilled in my brother and me to chase our dreams, and our purpose would be realized in time. I guess I always struggled to know what my purpose was, almost like my Dad or Mom should tell me. I did many things in my life to please them; I wanted to make them proud. Even though they constantly told me they were proud of me, I was looking for a sign that would guide me to MY destiny and purpose and not one that my parents hoped for.

I think my Dad sensed my confusion about what my purpose should be because I can distinctly remember when Dad and I went on a walk through the Piqua cemetery. The

Forest Hill Cemetery is located on the outskirts of town, near Fountain Park, which was my favorite park to play at growing up and his too when he was a kid. The cemetery used to scare me when I was younger, thanks to Michael Jackson's "Thriller" music video and all the moss-covered mausoleums and tall statues. One day, my Dad took me out to the cemetery and wanted to walk around and talk. He asked me my likes and dislikes and where I see myself in a few years; at that time, I was in 9th grade and just getting my bearings on being in high school, so I had no clue. I'm sure I answered in a way that would make him proud, not necessarily what I wanted to do. I distinctly remember my Dad stopping at one of the tallest and grandest mausoleums that I had ever seen, and he told me that the cemetery housed people with the most untapped potential and lost dreams. First of all, walking through the cemetery was scary enough, but I knew I did NOT want to end up like one of these people!

I was floored by his statement and the intense life lesson he was trying to teach me. It literally scared me, not only because of being in a creepy cemetery but also because I didn't know what having a true purpose meant at that time! Like how was I going to find this so-called purpose? Was God going to give it to me in a dream? Would I wake up one day and have this light bulb moment? Would I have this life-altering moment that would bust down doors? I wasn't sure, and my Dad also mentioned that he wasn't sure how and when I would receive my calling and purpose. He did express to me that when I found it, I would KNOW! I didn't understand what that meant at that time.

My Dad had his own financial advising business, and he is a great man to work with! I thought I wanted to follow him in the financial world; I even got my undergrad in Finance (boy, was that short-lived, lol). I soon realized that my one true love was Human Resources (HR), which Dad was happy with. He always told me to take baby steps, but he could see me as the lead HR Manager for a Fortune 500 company...but I digress; Dad was so good at what he did that he was always with a client or winning trips for his family to go on!

My parents had my brother and I traveling somewhere from an early age, and this is when I became interested in traveling and seeing more than my small city of Piqua, OH. Yes, I blame my love for traveling on my parents! But even more important, I credit them for pushing me to chase my dreams! We all want someone (especially loved ones) to rally behind you and push you to be the better version of yourself.

# CHAPTER 3:

## *"Don't Stop Believin'"*

-Journey

I have always wanted to explore our world and dive into different cultures, languages, and yes, the food! Every time I go to a different country while on vacation, I would come back home wanting more and quite anxious that I would have to return to the monotony and stress of work life. The insatiable wanderlust was slowly taking over.

I am a true dreamer; I especially love to drift off into space and daydream about my future! My Mom could tell you that I am always thinking ten steps ahead and need to slow down and enjoy the now, which has been hard for me.

I remember a story my Dad told me about not making the varsity basketball team because a coach told him his grip and shooting skills were no good. All summer long, he worked on his technique, took constructive criticism, and stepped his game up to get on varsity the next winter. My Dad is a firm believer that your words either would uplift you or defeat you; he would put affirmations all around the house. Some said, "You are Above and not Beneath, You are a Conqueror and not Defeated", so I took it upon myself to make my own affirmation. It read: "You WILL travel the world and see new things! You WILL pursue and chase your dream! You DESERVE to have your dreams come true! NOBODY CAN STOP ME!". Reading this daily helped boost my confidence, not only in my dream but in myself.

Let me tell you what the power of NO can do to a determined person. I remember sitting in one of my performance reviews, and my District Manager told me I would fail if he gave me a promotion at the time. I was stunned and furious at the same time, but I just smiled and nodded my head. Human Resources is one of my passions, and no one was going to tell me that I couldn't do it, and I didn't really want to deal with the politics within the workplace. Even my brand-new illustrious Masters' degree would not help me get promoted; I had grown discontented and did not even realize it!

So naturally, I looked elsewhere and started interviewing with another company. Their interview process was lengthy, but I was breezing by until the last interview...their corporate team said I didn't have enough HR experience. The HR manager had to politely tell me how sorry she was, but she could not extend an offer as much as she wanted to! After I talked to that HR manager, I cried like a baby, right in Smokey Bones restaurant and all over my ribs, with my Mom left there to console me as usual.

# CHAPTER 4:

## *"Endless Love"*

-Lionel Richie and Diana Ross

My Dad and Mom's marriage was the pinnacle of success to me! I always looked up to them, and even though I know all marriages are not perfect, they were my kind of perfect! I grew up in a loving and supportive home with two parents who deeply loved each other and us kids. I knew how important God and going to church meant to them and was at the foundation of their strong marriage, so I knew every Sunday we would get up and get ready for church. The church could hold a couple of hundred people in the sanctuary, the sanctuary was towards the front of the building, and if you made your way to the back, you would find many different rooms and an office. I spent time back in those rooms for Sunday school and helping with the little kids or babies. The outside of the church was white and had lots of grassy areas for the kids to play in and a creek in the back. The church was often like our second home since it was a huge part of our lives. My Dad would even preach a sermon or two if needed, as he was an ordained minister.

My Dad also made it clear that my Mom came before us.

Now some of you may be scratching your heads, and I didn't fully understand when I was younger, but now, as a grown and married woman, I get it! I distinctly remember when my younger brother, who looks like my Dad, and I were bickering with my Mom about something in the kitchen, and my Dad heard us from the other room; he came into the kitchen and told us to stop and respect my Mom's wishes and don't ever talk to his wife like that. I was like, but that's my Mom, and he repeated himself again, "that's my wife, and you will respect her." In my teenage brain, I didn't understand, but now I do.

There was a hierarchy in my family: God, wife/husband, then kids. I have seen so many people get divorced after their kids go to college, and I believe that is because they put so much of themselves into their kids and neglect their spouse that they look up one day and think, "who is this person?". My Mom and Dad were like plants; they kept watering their foundation (dirt) so that their marriage (stems) could flourish and stay strong enough to bear fruit (their children). My Dad would always praise my Mom, but also make suggestions and give her advice, as he did with all of us. He did so with love and encouraged our personal growth.

My Dad and Mom had a playful aspect to their marriage, which my Mom has often told me that helped keep their marriage fun. I remember walking into the house one time, and my Dad was chasing my Mom around the kitchen island, and I told them to get a room with disgust on my face. On the inside, I was beaming with pride because I had a great example of love and being in love with your life partner. Some of my friends didn't have this example, and I believe that is why many of them gravitated to my family. A lot of them consider my parents their pseudo parents as well, which I gladly share!

My Dad always exalted my Mom and made sure she felt loved. He always mentioned that he had a Proverbs 31 woman, so of course, I had to read that chapter in the Bible because I wanted to be like my Mom! Let me tell you why I wanted to be like her...she has the most gorgeous smile, makeup beautifully done all the time, matching outfits from head to toe, God-given grace, and so caring and giving. I remember I wanted my hair cut just like my Mom and I went through a bang stage and even had the Glamour Shots to prove it. So, when I looked up Proverbs 31 in my Bible, I was amazed because it was like they were describing my Mom! In current terminology and understanding, they discuss a virtuous woman who provides love to her household AND herself. A faithful wife, mother, and friend, she is willing to share her talents and gifts with them as well. I mean, this sounded like my Mother through and through! I even wrote a story about my Mom and becoming a Proverbs 31 woman when I was in grade school! I just KNEW I wanted to be like her but in my own way. I was headstrong even from an early age, but I always desired to have my Mother's grace. I would often watch her, and how she treated other people, and even if she were wronged, she was still loving. Watching the interactions between her and my father revealed how much they loved each other and wanted to continue to build upon their foundation. Even if you are down and out, you still have that one person who is your biggest cheerleader through life. I knew I wanted that! I know now that you should know how you want to be loved and navigate your relationships and friendships based upon that.

# CHAPTER 5:

## *"Party Up"*

-DMX

Even despite all the negativity and stress that the job at the store put me under, I stayed because I didn't know any better. I still had to make money, right? I distinctly remember one store I was placed at that broke me. I knew the bad reputation it had, and honestly, I was scared about going there. The district manager (who didn't want to promote me) told me that I was going to this store due to my bubbly personality because this particular store needed more friendly engagement from the management staff. I was comforted a bit by his words because it confirmed that this was not punishment but a challenge. I didn't realize how much of a challenge it would be!

The city worked with the Company to revamp this new store. When I first got to my assignment, they were trying to give it a facelift. The mayor, the head of the NAACP, and everyone else was excited at first, but most of the customers and associates were angry and unwilling to change. Nothing would or could be right in their eyes. I had never been assigned to a store that I had to deal with customer AND associate complaints EVERYDAY! It was taxing and draining. My bubbly and happy personality turned bitter and jaded, and I didn't like that one bit. I had started recognizing that my feelings for my best friend, Troy, who is a loving, sensitive, and fun person, were turning into something more, but I didn't have time to process them right then due to all the stress I was under.

(About five years back, Troy had friended me on Facebook one day, and I saw that we had a mutual friend, so I asked my friend if Troy was "good people" and made sure he wasn't crazy. She told me that Troy was cool, and I should accept his friend request, so I did. We talked on Facebook almost every day, which in turn ended up talking everyday via text and phone calls. We decided to meet up one day as we finally felt comfortable. We were almost inseparable after our first meeting, nothing romantic, simply good friends. Troy did express to me how much he would like to go further, but I wasn't ready for that. I didn't like him like "that."

We clicked, and I could see ourselves being good friends, but of course, he saw more. He even told me that in May 2009, when we met at the Troy City Park, he fell in love. I would ask him, you had love at first sight? I thought that was only in the movies. The funny thing is, we just walked around the loop at the park for about two hours, so nothing over the top or extravagant. I was just looking to have fun and meeting someone that likes almost all the same things I do, was awesome!)

After a long ridiculous day working, I would sit down on her brown couch, with a glass of wine, and tell my Mom about my day, and she would look at me in shock, and/or laugh because sometimes my stories just seemed so wild that they couldn't be true. I would have called Troy and told him all the craziness that was my work life as it happened.

For instance, on Christmas Eve, there were gunshots

going off near the building, but everyone kept working like nothing was wrong or happened.

"Ms. Jackson, Ms. Jackson. There are shots going off in the parking lot."

"Ok, are they shooting at you? Or someone else?"

"No."

"Ok, well, I am bagging these groceries. It's busy. Call 911. This is not the first time."

Another time I was told by a customer to go out to the parking lot and break up a drug deal; what do I look like? I was NOT about to walk outside and say, "Excuse me, sir, but could you please go sell your drugs on the other street corner? Thanks!".

Also, there was a time when a man followed me through the store and threatened to blow my head off. I had already asked him to leave the store, so he was mad. Mind you, we had security at this store, but most were worthless, and I ended up being my own security for the most part.

Finally, the man left only after I was on the phone with the police telling them that this deranged man was threatening to shoot me in my head. Of course, the police never came, but at least that did the trick to get the man away from me. I had to close the store on New Year's Eve by myself, which was terrifying. Being at that store taught me to keep scissors, a screwdriver, something in my car at that time. I have had men follow me to my car at night who would not take no for an answer.

Troy admitted that he used to drive down and walk around the store just to check it out and make sure I was ok. He never made his presence known, but he was watching out for me. I wish he would've been there this one night.

I remember it was the week before Christmas, and I got called to the register due to a customer complaining. Wait for this one...she was complaining because she could not use her competitor's gift card as a form of payment! Yes, you read that correctly, she wanted to use a form of payment that obviously I could not authorize. Of course, she became irate and told me that she should be able to use this form of payment because they are both grocery stores. I kept calmly telling the woman that she could not use this form of payment, and due to her creating a scene, she could leave the store if she doesn't have another form of payment. She proceeded to start cursing me out, calling me every name in the book. I started escorting her out of the building, and when we got to the lobby area, she turned back to me, and as I was starting to ask her to finally leave, I see her lean her head back, and then I see spit flying in the air towards me. Now, let me tell you, I am not one to fight, but I blacked out at that moment. I remember I started marching towards the woman, and I had my hands curled up by my sides. I was going to choke her, and as I got close to her, I heard the security guard shout, "MISS JACKSON, STOP"! It was like I was jerked awake; when I stopped and looked around, I realized that my hands were still curled up in a ball and ready to swing. The security guard got in between the customer and I, and he turned towards her and told her to get out of the building...NOW! All the while, she is still yelling at me and telling me to meet her outside after I get off work. In my head, I'm thinking, "lady, don't tempt me!" because the way I was feeling...I didn't necessarily have to wait until I got off the clock. I wanted to box her right then and there, I know it would've been a TKO (technical knockout) for sure!

So many associates came up to me and were saying, "dang, Miss Jackson, you have a lot of self-control" and "if it would've been me, you'd be kicking me out of the store too because I would've hit her." My head was swirling, pounding, and I was scared. I wasn't scared of that woman, but I was scared of what she almost made me do. Like I mentioned before, I'm not a fighter but don't push me! I have never once been so disrespected in my life! Have you ever been spit on? She did it so quickly and had no care in the world like I was some dirt that you spit on and kick around. I feared the thought of what I could have (and probably should have) done. I went upstairs to the manager's office, and just sat there. I didn't cry, I just sat there and stared at the wall for a minute and after a few minutes, I began to get angry. I was angry because I'm a highly educated, well-rounded woman, and I ended up in a grocery store getting spit on. HOW IS THIS POSSIBLE?

Since I was the closing manager that night, I couldn't leave the store for another two hours. I called my Mom, and that is when the tears came rolling down my face. When I told my Mom, she was shocked. She couldn't believe what I was telling her! She asked if I was physically ok and if maybe I should go to the hospital since there was bodily fluid involved. I felt so bad for telling my Mom because she always worried about us anyways, especially after my Dad died. I felt like I was giving her one more thing to worry about. I also remember calling Troy, and telling him about the situation, and he got quiet. I asked if he was still with me, and Troy said that he wanted to come down to the store, and see what was going on, just in case that woman did stay and wanted to jump me in the parking lot. Troy also stated that he couldn't wait for me to leave that particular store because he always worried about me being there. Shortly after this incident, I started suffering from stomach ulcers.

Weeks later, I had a conversation with my friend in church. She asked me if I had laid a hand on her, if I would have known when to stop, or if I would have stopped at all. I took a deep breath. I was so blacked out and had so much pent-up anger from my father's death that I am not sure. My friend said that even if the security was bad, in that moment, God was bigger. God had interceded and kept me out of prison.

It was the first time in a long time that I had to call off from work. I'm not sure if you have ever worked in retail but calling off work can throw off the day's productivity. I felt guilty for calling off. GUILTY! Why? I hadn't prioritized my own self-care and look where that is currently getting me! This painful sensation in my stomach, anxiety through the roof, gaining weight, and me turning into a jaded person who couldn't see up from down. I called off work to have tests done to find out why my stomach was hurting so much. Grief and work made me sick.

As I'm lying on the examination table, I'm worrying myself into an anxiety attack! I couldn't even put my focus on me for 10 minutes!?! I was worrying about what my co-workers were thinking, how worried my Mom and Troy were of me, and how I felt like I was letting my Dad down because I let myself get into this position. I kept apologizing to him again and again in my head, "I'm so sorry, Dad, I've let you down. I was trying so hard to take care of Mom and Paul, and I can't do a great job like you did for all those years". I don't know what made me feel like I had to be the one to take charge because nobody asked me to do that! I missed my Dad so much, with every beat of my broken heart.

# CHAPTER 6:

## "*Eye Of The Tiger*"

### -Survivor

Troy and I had become avid runners, especially once he realized that he would have to run to spend any time with me. We participated in numerous 5k (3.1 miles) and 10k (6.2 miles) runs, and one day I had the audacity to suggest that we were ready for a half marathon (13.1 miles). I told him, "It's ONLY 13 miles; how hard could it be?". Troy just looked at me like I had three heads but eventually said he would run one with me. When I told him my plan to get ready for this half marathon within a couple of months, he begrudgingly followed along. We would run all over the city, and we even ran from the outskirts of one city to the next, it was about 10 miles, and we thought we were hot stuff! Troy and I absolutely had no clue what we were up against!

I found a half marathon event in Indianapolis called Boomshaklaka; who wouldn't want to run that? It was later in the evening, around 7 pm on August 29, 2015. For some reason, I thought running at 7 pm in August was going to be a good idea. We enlisted my Mom's help because we didn't want to risk driving back home with sore legs. I drove us to

Indianapolis, and we were so excited because we prepared for this moment. The half marathon was supposed to be completed within 4 hours, and we chuckled because, of course, we would! We anticipated that it would take us about 2.5 hours to complete. When we pulled into the parking lot, we hopped out of the car and started getting our running fanny packs together and packed them full of rehydration gels. We didn't want to overheat and pass out along the way of the racetrack. We stretched out our legs and headed to check-in and then the start line. That is when my nerves kicked in. What in the world was I thinking? We have only trained for three months, and it is hot and humid outside.

As if Troy could read my mind, he grabbed my hand and said, "We got this, no matter what, we will cross the finish line together!". What confidence he exuded, which was so needed at that moment. I realized that this was my idea, but he was willing to see it through with me! When the buzzer went off for us to start, we started hand in hand. We would run a mile then fast walk one and as we would keep alternating Troy, and I would keep seeing this group of older ladies, and Troy was so determined to finish before them. I just wanted to keep pace and finish, whenever that would be, but Troy's competitive side had already kicked in, so I knew I was in trouble. Around mile 9, as we were running around a corner for the 1000th time, we heard a loud cry. Troy and I started to slow down as we were looking for where that cry came from and more so now that it was becoming more intense. We see an ambulance with its lights flashing and a marathon runner passed out in the grass on the side of the road. Every time one of the paramedics tried to touch her to get her in the ambulance, she would scream bloody murder. By this time, Troy and I had come to a complete stop to watch this scene unfold. We couldn't believe it, and I was more than grateful at that point to have Troy with me because that could have happened to me!

Well, needless to say, that moment mentally messed us all the way up. Our running pace and PR (personal record) were out the door. We couldn't get over the fact that something like that could easily happen, and we were more aware of how sore our legs felt. I told Troy at mile 10 that we could quit if he wanted to. He said that we should finish because if I were to quit now, I would be highly upset with myself the next day. Troy was so right in that assumption; I like to finish what I start. As we kept pushing, I noticed that there were less and less other runners. When we got to 12.5 miles, we gave it our last boost of energy and ran across the finish line while holding each other! The funny thing is we had to help each other cross the finish line, and that is when my thoughts were confirmed...we WERE the last ones to finish. We finished after three and a half hours, and even the photographer had left already, so the pictures I have from that event came from my Mom. My legs were so sore, and the event coordinator tried giving me ice cream, and I yelled out, "PLEASE GIVE ME WATER!". I was literally a hot mess after that run.

I'll never forget that half marathon though, it showed me that Troy and I could meet any challenge head-on and conquer it! It might take us longer than we anticipated, but we would get through it. So funny how life teaches us tiny lessons in preparation for the big exam. I am so glad I had these teaching moments throughout life to carry me through my grief journey and beyond.

# CHAPTER 7:

## "Address To The Stars"

-Caitlin & Will

I can never forget the day when my Mom and I were at the movie theater watching *The Help* when our Pastor was calling both of us to tell us to get home. When we did, we saw a police cruiser, and I immediately thought, "ooohhhhh, what did my brother, Paul do!?! He was not a troublemaker, but what else could it be? My heart started to sink, Mom became distraught and demanded answers, but they wanted to know where Paul was and said he should come home. Mom begged for information, but I knew in an instant what they came to say.

The conversation went something like this, "We're sorry to tell you that someone found Skip [my Dad] in his office on the floor. We're so sorry, but when we heard, we wanted to be the ones to tell you". When my Pastor and the police officer (who happened to be a good family friend) finally told us that my Dad was gone, it was like I had an out-of-body experience. In my head, I thought, "Excuse me? What did you just say?". Almost like in the movies when your spirit is floating above you and looking down upon your body. I remember telling family members about Dad's passing, and not a single person could believe it; it was too shocking! My Dad died due to a brain aneurysm; I pray that he didn't feel any pain. My Dad was active and an overall healthy man; why did this happen to him? Why was this happening to us? How could God allow a man to leave this Earth "before his time"? When he died, I felt like my tank was empty and that I was drifting. I didn't even know what my purpose was in life. He always believed in living a purpose-filled life and chasing dreams. I wanted to be like him.

So much grief and anxiety in my body led me to this doctor's office because I didn't know how to unpack my pent-up grief and stress, so here I am in this robe on a cold table getting an ultrasound. When I was officially diagnosed with stomach ulcers, I was angry, which of course, didn't help. My Dad had stomach ulcers when he was 9 years old due to his father's untimely passing as well. My ulcers were brought on due to unnecessary stress and anxiety, so I had to remind myself to breathe and think happy thoughts! It took the ulcer almost one month to go away and have me back at 100%.

# CHAPTER 8:

## "Why Don't We Fall in Love"

### -Amerie

I knew Troy still had feelings for me, but this time something was different for me. After *The Croods* movie, I found myself becoming more and more becoming more and more physically and emotionally attracted to Troy; I kept asking myself, "what is happening?", like I wasn't allowed to have those feelings. I remember looking at him one day during our walks, and something just melted in my heart. I was too hurt from past relationships and the loss of my father to say anything, so I kept it to myself. Almost like Troy heard my thoughts, he asked if he could take me out for a real date like a proper dinner and movie. Surprisingly, I said yes! Troy was my best friend, and I was starting to get over the way other men had treated me and hurt me in the past. I was on the phone with another guy who was being rude, so I told him to forget about our date, and guess who I called? I called Troy so fast, and he instantly agreed to go out with me that night. I know that had to have hurt his feelings to have been the second choice, and I remember my Mom even mentioning how wrong I was for doing that. She gave me that look, "I know I raised you better than this." Troy, later, told me how hard that was for him to hear that I was dating other men because he thought we were exclusive. That conversation was the turning point in our relationship. I put everyone else to the side and focused on Troy, and from then, I was all in! I just knew Troy couldn't be like that! Besides, it is just dinner and a movie; we aren't going to the chapel to get married!

When I think back to our first date, it was the most fun date I had ever had! I was totally myself, not putting on a front because he had already seen me when I was at a low point in life. When we got to T.G.I. Fridays and ordered food, I got a big juicy burger and ate it so fast! I'm quite sure I even ate the rest of his french fries and ordered dessert. When Troy and I look back at our first date, we crack up because he said he realized in that moment that I don't play when it comes to food. I thought I warned him that I'm not a dainty, strictly salad-eating type of girl. HA!

As many movies as we've seen together, I had never been to the Dixie Drive-in theater, so that is where we headed after leaving the restaurant. I could tell that Troy was so proud of himself for coming up with these plans. As we were watching the animated movie, *The Croods*, I just kept looking at Troy, and this sudden rush of emotion overcame me. He must've felt me staring at him, because he turned to look at me, and we moved in for our first kiss. It was so special because I felt safe with Troy, and it was special for Troy because he already knew his feelings for me, and now they seem to be coming to fruition.

I thought that we had been inseparable before, but since that night, it was even more so. Troy and I started seriously dating in the fall of 2013, but even then, I was still scared a bit. I was afraid of getting my heart broken and still reeling from my father's death, so I was one foot in and one foot out. Meanwhile, Troy is in the deep end and head over heels. I went away to Spain with a friend, and when I returned, Troy had purchased and gifted me a gold bracelet from Macy's. I was so surprised because no man has ever bought me such a thoughtful gift like that. Not only was Troy wooing me, but he also listened to me like truly heard me! When I would talk about future endeavors or things that happened in my life, he showed interest and cared. For instance, he showed up each year for the DreamChasers 5k event I have for the memory of my Dad. I remember Troy stating that he was so impressed by the amount of love that people showed my Dad, which made him love me even more.

As I mentioned before, my work life was becoming more and more overbearing, and with the combination of not properly grieving, I was becoming more anxious and perturbed with work and life, in general. These feelings took a grip on me, and I didn't know how to separate work and home life, so I would bring those feelings home with me and take it out on my loved ones. When all the crazy work situations would arise and finally when the stomach ulcers started happening, my Mom and Troy sat me down and asked me if I could ask for a transfer because I couldn't keep going on like this. I broke down crying because no one deserved to be treated in that manner, definitely not Troy.

# CHAPTER 9:

## *"Hero"*

-Mariah Carey

I was so angry. Angry at God for taking my Dad before his time, I was angry at my job for putting so much unrealistic pressure on us. I was also angry at myself because I felt like I was failing everyone, especially my Mom, Troy, and my Dad. I felt like I wasn't being as strong as I was "supposed" to be. I had gained 50 pounds, having bad eczema flare-ups, panic attacks, and my irritability was through the roof! I remember always apologizing to Troy and asking him, "Why on Earth do you stay with me?" and his usual response was, "because of my smile and big heart!". I knew it was going to be up to me to find that smile and joy again. I couldn't rely on anyone but myself to bring ME happiness and joy.

At that time, one of my favorite past managers called me up and asked how I was doing. Now, this particular manager was tough and hard on his management staff, but so many of them ended up moving on and up through the company because of the skills he would equip them with. He did have a playful spirit about him as well, but when it came down to business, he didn't play. I remember him calling me up one day, I was grocery shopping with Troy, and my old manager said,

"Hey Miss Jackson, I have a secret to tell you...you will be coming back to my store. I got you out of that current store, but you better be ready to work hard again, and you have to act surprised when your manager tells you later this week!"

I remember I stopped pushing the shopping cart and started crying! Troy runs over and asks what's wrong, and I told him nothing; it is great news! I thank my old manager, and I hang up with him, and as I'm telling Troy the good news, it just feels like I have air beneath my wings again. Like everything was going to be alright!

# CHAPTER 10:

## "Can't Feel My Face"

### -The Weeknd

Everything was alright for a while, but then I started noticing that I was slipping back into my old habit of complacency. I was even starting to resent the fact that I was still even working for this company. I didn't like the way management was treated by the corporate team and then how we had to trickle that treatment down to the store clerks. It was awful. After a while I was told that I was moving stores again, and this time I was going to my hometown store of Piqua, OH. I'm not going to lie; I was a little apprehensive due to me growing up there and wondering if the clerks would still view me as a little kid or if they would respect me within my position.

It didn't take long for me to figure out that even though I had grown up in Piqua, I didn't really know it at all. I saw some people and things that I never want to see again. I thought I had left one of the roughest stores in the region, but my own hometown store is almost as bad! Between the theft, people trying to scam the elderly via Western Union, people fighting, and oh that one horrible day that I was told to rush into the women's bathroom because someone was lying on the floor.

When I went into the restroom, I saw two bare feet hanging out of the stall, a woman's pants pulled down below her waist, her head near the base of the toilet with her hands sprawled out by her waist, and then my eyes went to the needle by her hand. I pounded on the door for this woman to open and of course it was locked. I proceed to crawl underneath the stall, praying underneath my breath that she wouldn't spring up and attack me! Might sound dramatic but based on movies and tv shows that I've seen, I knew people who looked dead might spring alive and scare you! While I'm doing this, I'm on the phone with 911 to get this woman some help, and once I crawled into the stall to unlock it, she started to stir and mumble incoherently. When the paramedics got to the scene, I got out of their way and they were trying to speak with her, and of course she couldn't really answer. One of them said the woman needed to be rushed to the hospital for an overdose. It was my first time seeing one unfold, but it wasn't that much of a surprise, since I knew Piqua and the surrounding areas had such a heroin drug problem. I'm not going to lie to you, seeing what that woman looked like lying on a public bathroom floor to get a high will always stick with me. I'll never understand what will lead people to want to do drugs, but I knew I never wanted to resort to that as a means to escape reality.

# CHAPTER 11:

## "God's Not Done With You"

-Tauren Wells

As if I needed another hint or sign from God, I specifically remember one day at the store when I KNEW it was time. It was like someone hit a gong and it reverberated so loud, like it touched my soul! I was at a new store and a new position within this store, I felt pressure because this new assignment was my hometown store. Facepalm, right? Working with some people I went to high school with or people who watched me grow up, and now I am their MANAGER can be quite awkward. There were times that I was told to reprimand specific associates, and I flat out refused. How could I do that, but then still maintain our friendship outside the building? I was always in charge of either the front-end department or grocery department, but at my new store I was placed in charge of the non-foods department. It is a smaller department, but the responsibility is still high...maybe even higher than the other departments. The tasks that were given to me, I extremely disliked. I am NOT Bob the Builder or Dennis the Display Maker, but that is what I was tasked to do, repeatedly. When I got to this store, it was time for a seasonal change which meant patio furniture needed to be built. Lucky me, right?

I know I can be a bit dramatic but let me set the scene for you...I started this particular shift at 8am. I had plans with Troy later that night, after I was to get off at 5pm so I told him to go to my house around 7ish and we could grab dinner and see a movie. I knew I was going to have to build some patio furniture, but other associates made it look so easy! I figured just me, and my Non-Foods Department manager can put together a couple grills and one or two sets of patio furniture, because how hard is it? Well, when 5pm rolled around, I believe we only had one grill, one swing, and half of a patio set put together. I tell Troy that I won't be able to leave until I get this done, but just wait for me. At 8pm, I tell Troy to get some food because we are having some trouble with this specific set.

While this is going on, I am growing more and more agitated and ready to throw myself a pity party! At around midnight, we started moving on towards a new patio set and we couldn't figure it out. It was at that moment when I stood up and looked at my department manager and told her that I was going to call my boyfriend and have him help us. I was tired and beyond frustrated. When I called Troy, I was crying, and just so mad and he told me to calm down and he would be there shortly to help. When I hung up with him, I knew that I needed to get out of there! How many hints and signs did I need to have, to get the hell up out of there? Up to this point, I had suffered from sleepless nights, stomach ulcers, intense headaches, irregular periods, anxiety, which I knew most of those symptoms were a result of losing my Dad but some of it was due to the pressures that work puts on store management. I just kept all the emotions and feelings bottled up, until they burst. At that moment, I almost dropped the tools I had in my hands and walked out. The only thing that stopped me was the fact that I had called Troy to come, and I was working with a sweet and caring woman, whom I didn't want to fail. None of this was HER fault, but we wanted to finish it together.

Troy came and looked at the hot mess of plastic bags, empty cardboard boxes, screws, and wrenches, halfway done patio sets, and a wobbly grill. I jumped up to give him the biggest hug and kiss, I don't think he realized at that moment how much he was saving me! Even though I hated this job and this task at hand, he made it seem alright. He started laughing and asking where to start because it was time for me to go home and sleep, his laughter and willingness to help melted my icy attitude. The three of us continued working and piecing together the rest of the patio sets that we needed. We listened to music and sang along, had a dance break at one point. It wasn't until about 3am that next morning, that we stopped building and decided to call it a night. I had been at that store for almost 20 hours, and all I wanted to do was get in bed.

I remember apologizing to my department head, for my lack of building skills and if my attitude had offended her in any way. She told me that it was ok and that one day we will be able to laugh about this moment in the future. I didn't believe her, but she was right. Whenever the three of us see each other, we often bring it up and laugh hysterically about it. It brought us closer, and we got to see a vulnerability, that maybe we were reluctant to show anyone else.

I felt like I had finally met my match, the one who gave me butterflies and made me giggle, but also the one who might be able to get me to "settle down", at least my version of settling down. Troy let me be, me! He enjoys my open and strong mind, and the fact that I can book a flight and pack my backpack and be gone, with no hesitation! He encourages my love for travel, even if it is something that he doesn't fully understand. I believe that it was six months into dating that I told him that he would have to get a passport if he saw this relationship lasting a long time. I told Troy that he would literally get left behind if he didn't get a passport. That is how much I loved to travel. Troy just gave me a blank stare and said "ok if that's what I gotta do to be with you. What do I have to do? How much does it cost?". I remember pushing and prodding him on different topics, such as religion, travel, and race in the beginning of our relationship to test him and see how far I could push him. Why? I guess the main reason is because of the fact of how much my heart had been broken in the past. I know you shouldn't look in the past, but oftentimes I cannot help it.

After two days of feeling bad for myself, something woke up inside of me, a dream that I had pushed to the side a long time ago. I decided right then I would stop crying, and do something for ME, quit my job and accomplish my long-lost dream and hopefully fulfill a deep desire within my heart. All dreams are different, and no one dream is too small or too big, just taking the first step is the hard part! Remember that you are more powerful than your boss, coworkers, family, or friends' no! I knew my heart's desire and my YES, was bigger.

# CHAPTER 12:

## *"Runaway"*

### -Janet Jackson

Early on in our first conversations, I had mentioned to Troy about finally using my savings to embark on a solo travel adventure and hopefully gain some clarity on exactly what Ashley wants and who Ashley is, he was all for it. Troy wanted me to do whatever it took to become a better person and feel whole again. Let's face it, the world does not stop turning while we're grieving which can make grieving hard! Even though my world stopped, and I was trying to catch my breath, it's like everyone gets to go on with their lives like nothing has happened! I know I am not the only one that has had this feeling!

What I admired about Troy, is the fact of how much he wanted me to be whole! He wanted that carefree and fun-loving person back. Troy wanted me to be physically, mentally, and spiritually ok so that I could function at my best, and if that meant I needed to go thousands of miles away, then so be it! His only request was that I make sure I book a return ticket. Most men probably would've said "oh no you aren't going nowhere solo!". Troy knew that I could handle myself and he even joked about how he would feel bad for anyone that would cross my path with negative energy or intentions.

Troy was taking a huge risk with me! I could have gone overseas and fallen in love with another man or country and decided to stay, but he was so confident in the way he loved me that I would come back! I know it sounds cliche, but I've literally not felt this kind of love before. I believe his confidence in the strength of our relationship is what led him to be so supportive of my crazy, adventurous endeavors. Troy would have lost it all, OR gain way more than he ever could've imagined. Have you ever had someone take a gamble on you?

Troy kept reminding me of how much our relationship means to him and that he truly hoped I would come back with clarity and peace. That type of support has been unmatched, besides my parents. I always say that I have the best hype man and cheerleader rolled into one! Sometimes the person meant for you, can be right in front of you and you don't realize it. I'm glad that I figured that out before it was too late.

Growing up, Troy didn't really get to celebrate his birthday since it was so close to Christmas. During our relationship, I have changed that and since I love to celebrate, I decided to celebrate him and his birthday before we were to leave for California for the start of my "World Purpose Tour". I invited our mutual friends and family to meet at my house and when we walked in the door, he was surprised and overwhelmed. I wanted Troy to feel just as special as he made me feel! A couple days after his surprise party, we were on an airplane headed for Los Angeles. I think we were both nervous, yet excited. We were headed for the big moment that I was going to be embarking on my journey!

I will always be thankful for and to Troy for his support, love, and understanding for this part of my life. If you have suddenly lost a parent, or any loved one, you know the unresolved questions and thoughts you have. Those answers may never come, but you will have to find a way to work through your grief and it won't be cookie cutter. I can honestly say it has been helpful having a great friend and love in my life to help me work through the pain that left a hole in my heart. Troy helped make my days as happy as possible, and for that I will always love him.

Don't even get me started on leaving my boyfriend of two years in the airport...I'm such an ugly crier! He's so supportive though, told me how proud he was to date a dream chaser and such a strong woman. Up until this point, I had never dated anyone who was so understanding and willing to give me space to be ME! When I was telling people about my plans to go abroad for an undetermined amount of time, they always asked "Well what about your job? What about Troy?". In my heart, I knew I couldn't stay at my job and be happy, but I KNEW Troy and I would be ok. Crazy huh?

Troy and I had a long weekend to ourselves in Los Angeles before my departure flight, which I am so glad we decided to do. We walked around Hollywood Walk of Fame, so Troy could see his favorite celebrities' stars and watch a movie at Grauman's Chinese Theater, we visited CityWalk by Universal Studios, we went to taco trucks (which I miss the most). We even went to a LA Lakers game, because one of Troy's dreams was to see Kobe Bryant play. Kobe Bryant was an inspiration to Troy, and since I was going to start chasing my dreams, so was Troy! We planned my departure from the States around a date when the LA Lakers would have a home game that we could attend. Troy and I remember Troy was so heartbroken because he had waited so long to see his favorite athlete play, and Kobe Bryant couldn't due to an injury. Troy and I talked about how we shouldn't keep waiting in life to do the things our heart desires! Unfortunately, Troy never got to see his favorite athlete play basketball nor see his daughter's namesake because he unexpectedly died in January 2020. Another reminder for us to live intentionally each day!

I'll never forget when Troy and I got dropped off at the LAX airport; he was going back home to Ohio, and I was headed to Fiji to start my big solo adventure! It almost felt like something out of a dreaded dramatic romance movie, I cannot stand romance movies (insert eyeroll). Little did I know, I was watching my own romance story play out. We sat on the airport floor, while I was charging my devices so that I could endure my upcoming 15-hour flight. I had never been on a flight for that length of time, I had my laptop and phone charging so I could be ready! I just knew that music and reading were going to get me through this flight!

While we are sitting on the airport floor, Troy and I talked about my travel plan that I had made so far; I was going to Fiji, then New Zealand and Australia. It would be the farthest I've ever been away from home at that time. I was so excited, because I was going to get PADI (Professional Association of Dive Instructors) dive certified in Fiji and then scuba dive in the Great Barrier Reef in Australia, which was a big bucket list item for me at that time. I had always likened myself to be a mermaid, the African American version of Ariel, Disney's Little Mermaid. I wanted to swim with the fish and maybe a whale shark or Great White shark? Yeah, I'm a bit too adventurous sometimes, but I wanted to see a different world than what I could see from land! Do you have a desire to do something that may seem dangerous? Some people already thought that a black woman traveling solo was dangerous enough, but not Troy! Troy encouraged it, he told me to go do what I NEEDED to do and come back "whole". This wasn't a *Eat, Love, Pray* trip, this was a lost soul going out into the world and trying to find that spark and twinkle in my eye that I once had. Troy realized that I couldn't be the best me, without hopping on that plane and taking this adventure. He told me to not listen to any of the naysayers and to chase my dreams, like my Dad would have wanted me to!

My heart had wanted to go on this adventure and have some breathing room, it felt like the right thing to do. When it was time to go our separate ways, it was hard. I had dated this man for two years and all the sudden I was going to just leave? Yes, I was geographically leaving him, but emotionally I was not. I knew he didn't want to let me go as we said our goodbyes, but he also knew that he needed to let me go. If he hadn't let me go, who knows where I would be today? If our love would be this strong? If I would be this strong?

When we had our final hug goodbye, it felt so quick and long at the same time! That last hug I gave him was so full of words that I couldn't form to verbally say, but I will say them now...*Troy I love you, I can't believe you trust me to go AND come back, you are such an amazing man and maybe I don't deserve you, thank you for allowing me this time to heal myself, I hope we stay true to each other while I'm gone but I will understand if not, I've never felt so broken in my life but thank you for coming on this heart's journey with me.* Troy and I didn't cry when we departed each other, we kept saying that "thugs don't cry" (his favorite rapper is Tupac). We both knew in our hearts that we would be ok, but it was still a long stretch of time to be without your significant other, and he had no guarantee that when I did return that I would still be his. Faith and hope, that is probably what got him through those nine months I was gone.

We both admitted to each other that we cried on the airplane to our respective destinations. When I first boarded my flight, I was excited and flipped through a couple pages of my book, *Eat Pray Love*, and fell asleep. I remember when I woke up and it was during the first meal service, and I was so excited because I needed a drink! While I was sipping on my wine, the Janet Jackson song *Runaway* came on my random shuffle. I started crying after listening to the lyrics as Janet Jackson described going all over the world, and she still found no one like her man. It hit me in that moment that I had really left Troy for a self-discovery world trip, but my love for him was unwavering.

# SECTION 2:
## *Travel*

# CHAPTER 13:

## *"One Love"*

-Bob Marley

My Dad never really wanted to get his passport or go out of the country. I would tell him that there was so much in the world to see, but he wanted to go to Las Vegas. Well, I ended up getting my Mom's passport for her and I told my Dad that we were going to go to Jamaica. My Dad was surprised but told us to have fun. Mom and I stayed at an all-inclusive resort, and we had so much fun. We ate, drank, went to the beach, and the pool. We went on an excursion to Dunn's River Falls, and I was so proud of my mom for climbing the falls because she is not the best swimmer, nor is she as adventurous as I am, but she wanted to participate and be there with me. My Mom had the most fun going to the markets to pick out different trinkets and souvenirs to bring back home. I remember one day as we were laying on the beach, my Mom was having a conversation with my Dad on the phone. My Mom was telling him how beautiful Jamaica was, how well I planned everything, and that she wished that he could be there. She then handed me the phone, and my Dad said, "Hey, when y'all get back go ahead and submit my paperwork for my passport, we're going to go somewhere. Your Mom really loves being out there, so I'm gonna get my passport". I was so elated! We finally got him onboard to get his passport!

When we returned home, I got his paperwork all submitted, and I even did a rush order on his passport. Dad got it in June of 2011, and he decided on going to the Cayman Islands, so I was planning our family trip to the Cayman Islands in January or February of 2012. Unfortunately, he was never able to use his passport because he passed away in September 2011. This is another reminder to truly live how you want to each day, because you never know when your time is up. You never know when you will take your last breath. My Father never got to use his passport, but we take it everywhere we go with us, and take pictures on the beach, so that his footprints are in the sand with ours.

# CHAPTER 14:

## *"Leaving On A Jet Plane"*

-Peter, Paul, & Mary

The plane ride from LA to Nadi, Fiji was about 15 hours long, up until this point, that had been my longest flight ever! I cried, I read a book, I slept, I ate and drank, then I would cry some more. I cried out of fear of the unknown, I cried out because I left Troy, I cried out because I hadn't had a chance to cry for my Daddy. That 15 hours was the longest of my life, and then we landed. I had never been out of the state nor country by myself before, so a wave of anxiety and wonder hit me at the same time! I was anxious because I wasn't sure what to expect and I'm such a planner, but the feelings of wonder and amazement took over! I DID IT! I flew overseas by myself, just like I said I would!

I headed to my hostel in a taxi, which I had never stayed in before! The only idea of a hostel I had was the horror film *Hostel*, which I refused to watch. When I arrived at my hostel, my worries drifted away like seaweed in the ocean. You could walk out to the ocean from our hostel and palm trees were everywhere! I immediately set my items down on my bed and locked up my valuables, so I could eat and call Troy and my Mom! I soon realized that you could meet all kinds of people at hostels, and you can be as sociable or antisocial as you want! Well, everyone who knows me, knows that I know no stranger! It was nice to meet new people and share our travel itineraries and stories.

I started my journey in Fiji for the main reason of wanting to become PADI dive certified; well, little did I know that January is cyclone season. A couple days before leaving the States, I got an email stating that my dive school is cancelled due to unsafe weather. I took it like a champ and decided to make the most of my stay in Nadi. The capital city of Nadi is somewhere that you only spend 1-2 nights in before leaving to go island hopping. Nadi is not the most picturesque town, like what you see in postcards and photographs of Fiji. I was due to be there for 6 nights because of the dive school, but I met the most incredible people and got to go snorkeling and see beautiful creatures at the Castaway island, like where Tom Hanks shot his iconic film! As a huge movie buff, I was so surprised that I never knew that it was a Fijian island that he was on!

The snorkeling was so magnificent on this island and the coral was remarkably close to the shore, which I've never encountered before, and I've snorkeled throughout the Caribbean. The funniest thing about this excursion is the fact that our tour guide dropped our group on the deserted Castaway island with nothing but a cooler of Fiji Bitter Beer! He didn't return for almost three to four hours, so basically if we were left to die, we were going to go out with a party!

That night our small group decided to go out and party in town. It was so cool to sit there and look around at our group; it was made up of all different nationalities and races: English, Scottish, Australian, Italian, German, and African American. Despite all that can happen in your travels, good or bad, at this moment after my fourth or fifth shot of tequila...life was GREAT!

The day I left Fiji, I was so sad to leave the new friends that I had made, but the beauty of it is most of us were following the same path to New Zealand or Australia! While boarding my flight to Auckland, New Zealand I noticed that my feet were starting to swell up, but I chucked that up to my lack of water intake in Fiji, I'm quite sure I only had one bottle of water. During the flight they got worse, especially my left foot. I took my left shoe off and propped it up because the pain became unbearable. The nicest couple that sat next to me on the flight kept asking if I was ok while we would talk about their home country of Czech Republic. Once we landed and I went to stand up, I fell back to my seat. I could not stand on my foot nor walk! The couple who sat next to me; I call them my Guardian Angels, came to my immediate rescue. They didn't even know my name, but they helped me get in a wheelchair and helped me through security and customs which was embarrassing! I was crying from the airplane through customs, and while waiting for our bags due to the kindness of this couple. We didn't formally introduce ourselves until we got to baggage claim.

The couple got me a SIM card that would work in New Zealand, and I looked at the wife and told her that I needed to go to the bathroom. I was mortified because she literally had to help me up from the wheelchair to the toilet seat. I wasn't going to ask for help, but it had gotten to the point where if I didn't go to the bathroom now, I was going to have an accident. I remember her shutting the stall for me to have some privacy and I knew she was waiting for me to finish, which was even more embarrassing. The couple asked if I wanted to be dropped off at the hospital and I refused, because I was going to prop my foot up in hopes that the swelling would go down. I didn't feel the need to go to the hospital, besides, I didn't need a hospital visit! So reluctantly, they drove me to my hostel. I had to hobble down a long corridor alongside the husband, to get to the reception area of the hostel. I remember the husband setting my backpacks down and telling me that he wished me the best of luck, and if I wind up in the hospital, please contact them again. I told him that I would be fine, but I'd let him know. I hobbled down the hallway to my room and within another hour or two, I noticed that my foot was gradually getting worse! I asked reception to call an ambulance because I cannot foresee myself being able to walk extremely far, and that is when I realized that New Zealand ambulances don't come for "minor" situations. I had to ask one of the hostel workers to drive me to the hospital, again all of this was so embarrassing!

I couldn't even walk so a couple of the hostel workers found a roller chair to put me in and wheeled me to the back of the building where there was an elevator. When I noticed that there was a gap between the building and the car, I asked for assistance to get me from the chair to the car. I was at my heaviest weight at this time, and I was mortified to ask anyone to help carry my weight. I was ashamed and mad at myself for letting this happen, even though I had no control over it! I remember I kept apologizing and making sure that my items would be safe in my absence since I had to leave some of my personal items back at the hostel, not knowing how long I would be gone.

I never imagined I would be admitted to the hospital because I never get THAT sick! I can't believe how many people I saw waiting for a doctor. I remember being able to tell them my name, show my passport, and what was wrong with me; by the time we got to the emergency room, I was in so much pain and it made my mind quite hazy. The hostel worker told me; people get called back to be seen by the doctor based on how serious each case is. I'm sitting there in excruciating pain, not able to walk, and thousands of miles away from my family and Troy and thinking what have I done? Thankfully, I only had to wait about 30 minutes, before

I was called back to the examination room. It seemed like an eternity. Little did I know that after the exam was done, they would tell me that I had a bacterial infection called cellulitis that was profoundly serious because it had gotten into my bloodstream, which came from a scrape by coral or nasty mosquito bite. At that point, it had become life threatening, but still I figured they would hook me up to a couple IVs for pain and antibiotics and then I could leave. I didn't realize that I was going to have to stay for a while, like eight days.

Trust me I was scared, crying, and calling out for my Mommy...yes, a grown woman called out for her Mommy! Imagine me, in a foreign hospital with no one I knew around! I was depressed and anxious. I had never been admitted to a hospital, and now I'm about a 22-hour flight away from home! How is this possible? I'm supposed to be on this grieving and "find myself" trip, and I end up in a hospital!

During my stay, I was able to cry, meditate, and pray, which I clearly needed to do. I prayed that the Lord would give me my Mom's grace and my Dad's strength, and more importantly healing and peace. I remember about halfway through my stay, my Mom asked me if I wanted to come home and I said no! She said, then stop crying and focus on healing so that you can go on with your dream trip! You've worked hard for this and don't let this hospital stay, stop you from achieving your dreams. At that moment, I knew that I was going to move on with my trip, sometimes you just need some confirmation from loved ones! I did let my Guardian Angel couple know that I was in the hospital, and they told me to stay strong and when I was released to let them know and maybe they could arrange a day to come pick me up and take me around Auckland.

Around day 5 of my hospital stay, I was introduced to a physical therapist. Even though the doctors had gotten the infection under control, my foot was still a bit swollen, and it was difficult and painful to walk. I worked with a physical therapist for about three days with crutches and exercises for my foot. Finally, after spending eight days at the Auckland City Hospital, I was released with crutches and antibiotics and a warning to stay out of the water until I finish the medicine. "But what about the Great Barrier Reef", I said. The doctor replied, "that will be a big no"!

I was finally released from the Auckland City Hospital after eight lovely (insert heavy sarcasm) days. Before I could even leave New Zealand, I had to stay with a lovely Kiwi (New Zealanders) family! They accepted me into their lives and made sure I felt comfortable and was doing my exercises. I even got to make them nachos one night, which they loved! Let me tell you, it is ridiculously hard to find Mexican dishes in New Zealand, but we improvised the best we could! I got to try vegemite, which is not for the faint of heart, let's just say I won't ever eat it again, as it has such a bitter taste, and I threw the toast out! This couple was planning their wedding while I was staying with them, and they even let me try their wedding cake samples and help them choose their flavors. I still joke with them to this day about getting a piece of their wedding cake and if they make nachos. I felt like I had been truly accepted into their daily lives, as they would call and check on me when they went to work. I wish I would've been more mobile because they wanted to take me to go hiking and other activities. I still was in contact with the Czech couple that helped me in the airport and when I told them where I was staying, they told me that they would pick me up for a beach day to get me out of the house.

They stayed true to their word and came to pick me up and took me out for a beach day. I mean it was perfect weather, perfect beach, the only thing that wasn't perfect was the fact I was still using crutches. Even the slightest bit of pressure and weight on my foot, would send a shooting pain up my leg. I hobbled along the grass to enjoy the picnic that they had prepared. We sat with another couple that were mutual friends, and I listened to them discuss how much housing was in New Zealand and how hard it was for banks to give out loans. I was listening to them, but all the sudden I heard The Notorious B.I.G.'s song "Hypnotize", blaring from someone's car. I was taken aback because it was crazy to see, or in this case hear, how widespread rap culture reached all over the world. I was snapped out of this revelry by someone asking me how the housing market was in the USA.

When we left the beach, the Czech couple took it upon themselves to show me around downtown Auckland via car since I couldn't walk around very well. As we made our way to the Auckland Space Needle area, we kept passing by picnics and it intrigued me because it wasn't a holiday or weekend. I asked the couple if this happens often, and they mentioned that they were probably the Maori people gathering. I was even more fascinated now, as I've never heard of them before. The Maori people were considered the indigenous Polynesian people who were voyagers that settled in New Zealand. When the Europeans started colonizing New Zealand, they started stealing land from the Maori people (no big shocker here!). The Czech couple told me that the Maori have been fighting for their rights and their land, and the New Zealand government was gradually giving it back. They get certain things for free, such as school, use of parks, etc. It was the first time that I heard about colonization outside of Native Americans and slavery with my ancestors.

The couple eventually pulled over and helped me hobble to an area that had Maori statues. Looking at these statues with other tourists was so surreal. They told the story of the Maori people and how they sailed the blue ocean and decided to settle in New Zealand, not that I could blame them! From what I could tell, New Zealand was a beautiful country with some nice people. Like I mentioned before, this was the first-time seeing colonization outside of my own country and it impacted me. It made me realize that this happened all throughout history to different cultures. What made one set of people think it was ok to go find some land that was already inhabited and essentially kick out the indigenous people? What is the thought process behind this? Those are questions that I kept pondering throughout my journey and even still to this day!

I appreciated the Czech couple for showing me around that day and I knew that one day I would return to this fascinating country. Once I felt strong enough to move onto my next destination of Australia, I was both sad and happy to leave New Zealand. New Zealand taught me that it's not necessarily the terrain and landscape that I should be focusing on, but the personal relationships that I can find and build with people which is more everlasting in the long run! I tried preparing myself for this trip the best way I could, but obviously you can only prepare for so much. Life happens and it's how you deal with it that determines the outcome! Just keep pushing through and don't live your life with regrets!

# CHAPTER 15:

## "Lean On Me"

-Bill Withers

The love and support continued after leaving Auckland and throughout my stay in Australia! I started my Australian adventures in Sydney, then went to Cairns, and finally Perth. I found multiple people who were willing to help me along my journey and each person has a special place in my heart! I stayed with a friend that my Mom's boss had met a long time ago while traveling, in Sydney. This lady took great care of me and drove me around to show me the Sydney Opera House and Sydney Harbor Bridge since I still couldn't walk around without being in pain. She even took me to a rowing house, and I felt like I was high society because as soon as you walked in you just felt rich. I was a tight budget backpacker, so you know I sucked that whole experience in! We sat on a balcony and just watched rowers in their boats, practicing for some competition, I'm sure. Meanwhile, I'm shoveling all the olives, cheese and crackers, and seltzer waters in my mouth, that I could! I knew I wasn't going to be able to eat like this all the time, so might as well take advantage when the opportunity presents itself.

The main reason why I wanted to go to Australia was to go to Cairns, which is where the Great Barrier Reef is located. Since I didn't become PADI scuba certified, due to the weather in Fiji, I was still determined to see the Great Barrier Reef by any means necessary! I found a glass bottom boat tour that would allow me to see the reef, but also stay dry since I was told by the doctors in New Zealand that I was not allowed to submerge in water yet. I had a great experience, the colors of the reef, fish, and water really made my surroundings look magical. It was like Finding Nemo, but in real life. The tour was also informative as I learned that the reef is dying and that there are nature groups trying to lobby for the end of tourism to the reef. I took it as another example of how humans don't take care of the Earth we live on and it takes a couple bad ones to ruin it for the rest of us!

The wildlife in Australia is beautiful but can also be dangerous. I remember reading about the deadly spiders, snakes, and bats. I recall one evening I was out with a friend I made in Cairns and she mentioned that we better get back inside her house before it gets too dark because large congregations of fruit bats will start flying. I had to look up fruit bats and I was appalled by the size of them, not one to normally get scared by bats but I was afraid of these vampire sized ones. This same friend also happened to mention that she saw a huntsman spider in her house a couple weeks ago and of course, I'm looking around like where did it go? Will I find it when I wake up in the middle of the night sleeping next to me? She said that they don't normally attack humans, but they are big enough to prey on other spiders and insects and move very quickly. I couldn't sleep my first night in Cairns for that reason. After leaving Cairns, I flew to Perth which is one of the biggest cities on the west coast of Australia.

I found an Airbnb that I wanted to stay in and since I couldn't get around still, I figured out how to use the Australian grocery delivery service! I thought I was the smartest person ever! A Swedish couple were staying at the same Airbnb as I was and saw that I had ordered groceries. At first there was a language barrier and a misunderstanding, but they really grew on me and we became fast friends. This couple was in Australia to do a working gap year, so they were trying to look for a job and an apartment to stay in. I thought that was so awesome, because back home after you graduate, you're expected to head off to college. After speaking to so many Europeans, I was starting to see that gap years were quite normal and encouraged! Meanwhile in America, you need to compete with your peers to get into an awfully expensive college, and hope that you can afford it or get scholarships to cover the costs, and then when you graduate compete with those same peers (plus more) to get a job. I was continuously keeping the differences in our ways of life in the back of my mind. Even though we have these different nuances, we are all still human, and need connection which is why I was (and still am) so thankful that this Swedish couple happened to be at this same Airbnb.

One of them was a physical therapist by trade, and once I told her about my story, which began in Fiji, she immediately told me about different exercises to try. She also told me that I would have to eventually start putting more pressure on my foot so that I could learn to walk properly again. Of course, I didn't want to hobble around for the rest of my trip, so I started implementing what she told me to. Once I was feeling a bit stronger, they offered to drive to a local beach, and I was all for it! I still couldn't get in the water, but it was so nice to see the beach and walk on the sand with my new friends.

One day they offered to drive me to the hospital in Perth, Australia for a check up on my foot. It was still a bit swollen, so I wanted to make sure that all seemed fine before my next destination of Bali. I didn't want to fly there and end up in a hospital in Indonesia! I had had enough of hospitals during this trip! On my last night at this Airbnb, we went out to a nice beachside restaurant where we could watch the sunset and have a glass of the famous Margaret River wine. Those are the types of moments that I sit back and think a lot about, like I really traveled solo the furthest I could from home and was still making friends in seemingly random places! Sometimes we didn't quite understand each other due to the language barrier, but we knew we had an everlasting friendship and would even consider them family. These are the types of friendships that I have been blessed to make all over the world. I thoroughly believe that somethings happen for a reason, and it brings you in the pathway of certain people. I am ecstatic to have met these people along my journey of life and can still call them my friends today!

# CHAPTER 16:

## "Best Friend"

-Brandy

When I left Australia for Bali, Indonesia, I was excited and apprehensive. I had never been to Asia before, and I wasn't sure what to expect. *Lonely Planet* guidebooks and Google searches can only get you so far, you must see it, hear it, and smell it! I was still using my crutches when I got to Bali, so I was one of the last ones to leave the plane so that I could use a wheelchair which by now I have totally gotten over being embarrassed riding in a wheelchair. I just knew my foot wasn't strong enough to handle me walking on for a long period of time. I was ecstatic to finally get to Asia and especially Bali because I was turning the big 3-0 on this continent.

I strategically planned to be here during my 30th year celebrations because I remember reading how cheap everything from food to clothing to nightlife was! Let's not get started with the famous and Instagrammable Bali spa baths! If you've never seen a Bali spa bath, just imagine a modern style foot claw bath made from stone, filled with warm water and beautiful flower petals just waiting and beckoning your name. I just KNEW I had to go there and spoil myself! I also would be meeting up with one of my closest friends, who had previously opened my eyes to travel and the experiences and knowledge that you can gain from traveling the world. I just want to take a moment and tell you about this friend. She is not only a force to acknowledge due to her height but because of her aura. She has a sense of confidence and determination that dims for no one, the full essence of a Leo woman. She is a fierce woman full of black girl magic! We have always seemed to be on the same wavelength in life and it is always an adventure when we meet up. When I called to tell her that I was quitting my job and going to travel, she told me that she was thinking about doing the same! When she mentioned that she would like to have her first group trip go to Bali, I was on board because that was going to be my first Asian country that I was going to visit on my world trip. Having her in my life was and still is especially important to me and something that I will always treasure.

I got there about four days before she did, and I remember participating in a couch surfing exchange for one night. Couch surfing is when you offer up your couch or bed to someone who is traveling, for free. The host may ask the couch surfer to fix meals or bring a special trinket that represents their country, or even just ask for language lessons. I stayed with a Balinese man, who barely knew English, but he offered to show me the local food stalls and way of Balinese life...not the commercialized version. Having this experience meant a lot to me because I liked to see how people "really" live and not necessarily the pretty version. Even in the man's broken English, he tried asking me about my experience as a black woman, and I tried telling him in the easiest way possible, but I'm sure something got lost in translation. Before I left, I was able to help him with some of his English skills as he said he wanted to learn more for his job. I'll never forget that man with the kind smile and open mind and heart.

My Mom, Troy, and my Grandmother had rented a villa for me to stay in for three nights, to bring in my 30th birthday in style! Before I was able to check in, I was picked up by an awesome tour guide and he took me to see rice fields, beautiful temples, I got to eat the best tasting nasi goreng (fried rice with meat) and tried luwak coffee which is made from partially digested fruit that was defecated by Asian palm civets. They are cat-like creatures that almost look like raccoons but are indigenous to SE Asia and many people will trap and sell them for their poo. Because of the rarity of the way the coffee is made, the luwak coffee is the most expensive coffee in the world. I was indifferent towards the luwak coffee because I was more excited about the different teas to try. My favorite tea was lemongrass tea, and as a matter of fact, I didn't even know what lemongrass was until I got to Bali and tried the tea. The smell of lemongrass and the refreshing taste of lemongrass kept me wanting more. It made me feel calm and I had never had a cup of tea that tasted so good. I know...call me adventurous or crazy because I'm a little bit of both! It was a day filled with wonder and amazement, at the busyness and beauty of Bali. How could something so pretty be so gritty at the same time?

When I was finally taken to my villa to check in and set my bags down, I was astonished and left speechless! The villa was gorgeous, and I had it all to myself! My bed was covered in rose petals that spelled out Happy Birthday, and it had this amazing dipping pool, which I couldn't wait to swim in! After my long day out with the tour guide, I decided to shower and venture out for dinner and along the way, I came upon a nice-looking bar called *The Red Carpet Champagne Bar*, and I just KNEW I had to celebrate my birthday there, because anyone that knows me knows that I LOVE champagne! I made reservations there for the next evening and got something to eat. That night, I rested very well because the next day I was turning 30 and I couldn't wait to celebrate myself and by myself! I was excited to celebrate myself and have some peace because at this point it had been five years since I had lost my Dad.

The next morning, the manager of the villa asked if they could come in and prepare my breakfast and I happily obliged! I couldn't believe how spoiled I felt, they made nasi goreng (which had become one of my favorite Balinese dishes) and even gave me a cold Bintang Radler which is a Balinese beer to go with my breakfast. I normally do not like beer, but what made this beer taste so good is the fact that they added lemonade to the beer. They sang happy birthday to me and everything! I felt so special. I had my whole day planned out and I couldn't have been more excited! I was going to spend the day at a highly recommended spa, getting the full royal treatment! It all started with a foot bath, then a massage, then Bali spa bath, then a facial, and finally a manicure and pedicure, and they even gave me a fruit plate and champagne to drink! Troy happily paid for this spa day as it was ONLY $50! Now back home in the States, that would have easily cost $400+ so it felt great to be able to have this moment for me! By the time I got back to the villa after my spa day, it was time to get all dolled up and go out to dinner. I'm sure people were curious to see me all dressed up and eating alone but I had gotten used to it by now in my solo travels. I sat up on the second level and there was an opening which looked out over the ocean and I could hear the raindrops fall. It was extraordinary to think that at this moment, I was by myself in a foreign country and celebrating my 30th birthday by myself and being OK with that!

I ended up at *The Red Carpet Champagne Bar* for my nightcap and dessert, and I was so excited to be there! Once again, I am there by myself and enjoying my time! All the sudden I heard 50 Cent's song "In da Club" started playing and I saw a few servers carrying champagne bottles that had sparklers lit and they crowded around me and were dancing. I hear a DJ saying my name and Happy Birthday. I was overwhelmed with joy and appreciation in that moment, not just because of this surprise of champagne bottles but little did they know that my Dad used to call me each birthday and play that song before he would come on the phone (or in person) and wish me a happy birthday. Yes, my Dad would listen to 50 Cent!

As I was trying not to cry into my champagne, an Australian woman came up to me and asked if I would like to sit and drink with them because in her words "you shouldn't drink alone on your birthday." I was so touched, so I said yes! There were two Australian couples, and they were so amazed that this American woman was traveling solo throughout SE Asia. I told them why I was traveling, and they empathized with me, Bali to them was a short flight away to paradise almost like how Americans view Mexico or the Caribbean, but to me it was a whole new world! A world that I loved exploring and finding myself in.

Eventually I had to leave my majestic villa because my friend was flying into Bali for her inaugural group trips that she plans. I was so proud of her for her turning her passion into something that she was building for herself and I had hoped to be able to find what I was passionate about and eventually start my own business. I was so proud of her for starting BeHUEmane and sharing her passion for minorities to discover the world and all that is in it. It was my first familiar face that I got to see and I'm not going to lie, I teared up a bit when I saw her. All that tension and anxiety that had built up during my time in the hospital and not having a friendly, familiar face to comfort me was finally released when I saw her. Going from traveling solo to having a friend with me was great, but I was a bit nervous about the group aspect since multiple people means multiple different ideas and concerns. I also had another friend from home coming on this trip, so it was going to be interesting to see the different dynamics of everyone and how well we would all mesh.

My friend planned a great ice breaker for the group and planned a hike up Mount Batur. Since I was just getting comfortable without using the crutches, I decided to opt out of the hike, but I still wanted to support the group, so I sat in the tour van while everyone else went up to the hike. It was around 4 a.m., so it was pitch black dark, and I was by myself in the tour van with low cellular reception, and I just had to wait for them to come back. Upon their return, my friend described the sunrise hike as one of the best and most beautiful hikes that she has ever been on. Due to it being dark outside still, the hike was a bit treacherous and steep, but the views were worth the trek. She described the clouds dancing across the volcanoes, amongst the mist, with the sun rising, and oh it sounded like a movie scene! I was sad that I couldn't see it but after she told me about it, I knew that my foot wouldn't have been able to handle the hike. Listening to the group's excitement about the hike and the upcoming activities that were planned, really made me realize that she accomplished her goal of breaking the ice and having the group come together as one.

I remember sharing my story with some of the group members and their reaction to me traveling solo and working through my grief of losing my father. They thought I was courageous to go out on my own, but I didn't see it that way. I just knew I needed to stretch my wings and breathe, and I felt stifled in my dead-end job and I felt like the world was calling me, so I reached out to answer! When I first told my friend about my plans to quit my job and travel, she was my number one cheerleader! Over the years since we graduated from college, we had started meeting up in different states and countries, and when I saw how life had progressed for her, it was nothing short of amazing. Like I mentioned before, I had hoped that I would and could find my own passions and purpose during this trip.

Bali was a beautiful sight to see! There were rice fields, jungles, beaches, and city life to see, there was something for everyone. The group got to walk along rice fields and ride on elephants. I had never seen myself riding an elephant, but it was so amazing. I had to fight with some monkeys in the Sacred Monkey Forest, yeah, those monkeys may look cuddly and nice, but they are grabby with shiny objects and get mean if you run out of food. In fact, one monkey peed on my friend, we just laughed hysterically about that because what else could we do? You must pick your battles especially abroad.

We also happened to be in Bali during their new year called Nyepi which is a weeklong celebration. The night before Nyepi parades and sculptures called Oogh Ooghs float down the street. Oogh Oogh are large scary looking creatures, that oftentimes will get burnt shortly after being seen in the parade. Then the next day, which is the new year day, is greeted with complete silence, even the airport is closed on this day, no flights going in or out. The silence is to provide you some space for self-reflection and mediating Between learning about the history of Bali, the new friendships being formed, and spa days, I knew it would be hard to leave this group of ladies.

When it was time for us to leave Bali, everyone else was going home and I ended up heading to Malaysia and beyond. I remember being anxious because two of my good friends and some new friends were leaving me. The journey I was on, constantly changed and moved and that was alright with me. If it felt good and right, then I was going to go in that direction because I was being led to. My Dad always told me to listen to my inner voice, my intuition and even though he wasn't there to see me, I felt his presence all around me.

# CHAPTER 17:

## *"Brown Skin Girl"*

-Blue Ivy, Beyoncé, SAINt JHN, & Wizkid

Now if you know me, I like my personal space and in Asia you don't get any! Having little to no personal space is something that I had to get used to. This is a learning experience for me, as I normally don't like people touching me or getting into my personal space. I eventually got more accustomed to it, as I knew I would have to learn which battles to pick especially since some people were attracted to me due to being a black woman. Something else I had to get acclimated to is everyone in SE Asia is in a hurry to get somewhere. I usually called it in a "hurry to go nowhere", because of how bad traffic is. We all were going nowhere at the same time. I thought Bali had a lot of traffic, but it was not as much as Bangkok, Thailand! All the tuk tuks, taxis, and scooters! Tuk tuks are usually three wheeled motorcycle taxis that clog the streets of SE Asia. They are cheap transportation, and you can always negotiate a price you want to pay before getting into one! 2-3 people could fit comfortably in one, but of course it was usually 4-5 people trying to cram into one so that we could split the cost which would sometimes end up being less than $2-3/person, depending upon your destination.

Despite all the traffic, Thailand is such a magical place. When I landed in Bangkok and took a taxi to my hostel, I was peering out the window in awe. It was about 1am, but it was amazing to see how many people were out! People out and about, walking around laughing, having a great time, and I remember being excited to explore Bangkok and hopefully meet some new friends. The whole taxi ride from the airport to my hostel, made me so excited to be there and I just had this sense of joy and anticipation! I didn't know what to expect but that also increased my excitement! I never thought I would have found three girls that I would have traveled with and become lifelong friends within Thailand, but that's exactly what happened!

I ended up befriending three girls; one was from Portland, Oregon and the other two were from Quebec, Canada, and we just so happened to be staying in the same room at the hostel. The next afternoon we went to one of the biggest malls in Bangkok, called MBK Center, and going there for the first time I was just in awe because it had eight levels. There were so many different stores to see, and I can guarantee that I never saw all of them! There were tons of different restaurant options in the food court, anything from smoothies to Chinese waffles to Thai food to Japanese food. Oh, it was such an amazing sight. We went there because of the heat and humidity outside so it was nice to get some air and eat some really good food. Also, walking around the mall, and getting lost in the different boutiques filled with anything from t-shirts to jewelry to phone gadgets, this mall had it ALL!

But at night walking around outside and gawking at all the delicious street food vendors was also a sight to behold! Street food kiosks in Bangkok are such a huge part of the culture there, and I loved trying new foods and eating what

I could. The pad thai was always amazing and the lady that would make roti with Nutella, banana, peanut butter, or honey was always a stop for me while in Bangkok! Thai roti was a sight to see being made! A street food vendor would take a normal plain roti bread and flip it and stretch it to perfection while frying it up in butter and oil then adding your favorite sweet or savory toppings to it! My favorite was peanut butter and banana, hey don't knock it until you try it! Plus, it was dirt cheap! I often think of that lady that would stand outside of a 7-11 convenience store flipping her roti and her gap-toothed smile. Hers were the best and served hot and delicious! Bangkok and the street food are what kept me coming back to Thailand, I used Bangkok as a jumping off point to maneuver throughout Southeast Asia because the flights were less expensive, and it was pretty much a gateway to all Southeast Asia. It was nice to have people there with me that I felt comfortable with, and we had grown close together, like fast friends. We would have deep conversations about why each one of us was traveling and what we wanted to do with our lives. I shared about my father passing, and one of the Canadian girls did mention that her dad had passed away as well when she was younger. It almost seemed like a badge that we carried that neither of us wanted, but we knew that we would, for the rest of time.

The girls and I spent a lot of time together, and we got to experience different cities throughout Thailand together, such as Chiang Mai, Chiang Rai, and Pai. At times we'd split up and do our own thing, but then we'd come back together and travel throughout Thailand together, which was special. At one point, I ended up going to Myanmar to see parts of the country since I was in SE Asia.

So, I am pretty used to getting looks, stares, pointed at, and asked for pictures in almost every country in SE Asia because of my hair and skin color, but Myanmar (Burma as the English call it) surely takes the cake as the most intriguing people. Myanmar has been shut off from tourism for so long, just as early as 2010 was it safe for people to freely engage with Myanmar. I arrived in Yangon, Myanmar the second to the last day of their water festival called Thingyan. I had previously been in Thailand during the beginning of Songkran, and I got drenched everyday all day, but Thai people have NOTHING on the Burmese people when it comes to the water festival activities. In Thailand it seemed more commercialized and gimmickier, but in Myanmar it was more about the rituals and people just having fun and anticipating a great new year!

Thingyan usually lasts about three to five days, and guess what...this year it lasted five just so that I could spend a few extra days getting drenched! LOL! It is customary to throw water on everybody that walks past, because it is seen as a cleansing ritual to prepare you for the next year. Only the elderly and monks are safe from this practice...although there were plenty of elderly who threw water on me but it's all in good fun!

I remember as soon as I hit the street early on the last day of Thingyan, which was my first full day in Yangon and people stopped dead in their tracks and just pointed. Now I mentioned before that I have seen this before, but the Burmese people were not shy! There were truckloads of people yelling for me, and I didn't even realize it until a group of tourists I was walking around with shouted at me to pay attention to the locals staring at me! I had so many Burmese women try to give me betel nuts (an addictive stimulant much like tobacco or caffeine) to chew and clay powder to put on my face, but I firmly had to tell them no each time. I even had one woman come up behind me, pull me back and try to forcibly put betel nut in my mouth! The Burmese people were not shy when it came to wanting pictures or just the obvious stares or finger pointing. I took a video of ONE man taking pictures of me with THREE different phones, now that just blew my mind!

I remember being in Bagan, Myanmar and getting ready to plan out all the temples I was going to tour that day. I saw on Facebook that the singer Prince had died. Prince was very influential on my Dad's musical choices and my Dad was one of the first people on his block to have the newest Prince records as he was growing up. The hostel I was staying at started playing his music in honor of his memory. I thought it was interesting since Myanmar seemed to have been cut off from the rest of the world, but it was another reminder how music defies boundaries and unites the world.

I initially went to Myanmar to visit a Buddhist monastery since that was on my bucket list, I spent four days at a Buddhist monastery called The Bar Wa Centre. Many people have asked me why I travel and there are many reasons, and one of my main reasons is that it is a humbling experience for me. Visiting the Buddhist monastery didn't disappoint! There was barely any cellular service, only got to eat twice a day, no meat, and running water would be cut off at random times throughout the day. You could be taking a shower and the water would stop running halfway through, leaving you to run outside in a towel with a bucket to fill it up and run back upstairs with it. Plus, visiting the infirmary area of the monastery, I remember looking around and wondering where all the wheelchairs, crutches, etc. happened to be and I was told that they couldn't afford to purchase those items for the ones who were sick. By this time, I wasn't really using the crutches and thought to myself, they needed to be left here at the monastery. I remember presenting the crutches to the monks there at the monastery and they couldn't wait to take pictures of me and with me.

By the time I got to Myanmar I gave up on trying to flatten my hair, so my curly afro was flying high and mighty! One woman told me that they would have to pay a lot of money for something that I have naturally, and the monks were so intrigued by my hair. It had been my dream to stay at a Buddhist monastery, and learn more about Buddhism and meditation, and these monks and nuns were asking about ME!?! All this ruckus because of me and my hair? I didn't know it at the time, but I was diving into a deeper level of self-love! I can't tell you how much I love my skin AND hair after my experiences in Myanmar! I believe this is the country, along with its people, that helped me appreciate my natural beauty, and realize that I can love the way I look and not conform to society's idea of what beautiful is! I love me, my black skin, and big afro! Afros and passport stamps forever!

That experience really humbled me and made me appreciate where my life was in that moment. I couldn't wait to get back to Thailand and see my friends again, so that I could tell them what happened. We all had stories to share, and I couldn't wait for them to know what I had been through and that I had FINALLY gotten rid of those pesky crutches! Getting rid of those crutches felt like a breath of fresh air and like a weight had been lifted from my shoulders. I'm so glad I left them at the monastery and that someone who needed them most would be able to receive that gift.

We visited Chiang Mai for the water festival, called Songkran, we visited the White Palace of Chiang Rai, and visited a hippie type of city named Pai. The White Palace of Chiang Rai was an adventure to get to, as we took scooters around to find the palace and it was like one of the hottest days ever! Walking around the White Palace was so hot, it was almost like the pure white made the sun reflect and heat our skin up even more. As we walked around and looked, we saw that the sidewalks were lined with bones and skulls which made it even more intense. How could something so beautiful be creepy at the same time? I still don't understand what that palace was a shrine to and I'm not sure I want to know. When we went to the city of Pai, we climbed up beautiful white stairs to see Wat Phra That Mae Yen or White Buddha Pai. The White Buddha Pai is where the picture of me was taken that is on the cover of the book! By this time in my trip, I had lost some weight and was feeling good, but that steep climb and multiple stairs knocked the wind out of my lungs. It took almost all my energy to climb the stairs up to see the Buddha, and I had to catch my breath, so I sat down. As I was catching my breath, I was able to look across the city of Pai and be amazed by how far that I had come, not only hiking up all the stairs but in life!

We even went to Songkran together. It was so much fun doing that in Chiang Mai, and all the water that was used... we got so wet. There was never a dry spot on us, and it was fun running through the streets with water guns and spraying everyone. There was a big music festival happening as well and even though we couldn't understand the music, we still partied and had fun. Being carefree, dancing in the streets while soaked with water was an amazing feeling and one that I will never forget! Everybody was so full of joy. When I reflect on it now, it really gave me life to be there in that moment on that street. In all my wet clothes, listening to different bands play, not knowing the language that they speak but music is universal. Music is so important to me, with all those car rides with my Dad that I used to take and how I still listen to that same music to this day. As if I feel connected to him through that music, like a portal. I'm so grateful for my time with those girls, and the love and friendship that we shared with one another, even after a couple weeks of traveling with each other. It was amazing that this could even happen. This is my life and I'm finally living it and enjoying it, without feeling guilty.

# CHAPTER 18:

## "*Miss You Much*"

-Janet Jackson

Where do I start? I fell in love with the place, with the WHOLE country! I loved the people, culture, history, and food. Also, the fact that I didn't have an income, and yet I could still live like a Queen there! The conversion rate between the US dollar and the Vietnamese dong is amazing! You automatically become a millionaire because one USD = 23,200 VND, so you know I was excited and instantaneously the thought of leaving this country made me sad.

Not only was it cheaper to live and stay there, but Vietnam has so many different landscapes! They have mountains and rivers in the North in Sapa an Halong Bay, then beaches near Da Nang in the middle of the country, plus you have busy (I do mean BUSY) metro cities like Hanoi in the North and Ho Chi Minh Saigon in the South. Hanoi and Ho Chi Minh are vastly different, and I'm not a huge history buff but I learned that The US soldiers were stationed in Ho Chi Minh. This made sense as to why the food, night life, and buildings looked different then up north and Hanoi.

I loved waking up in the morning and heading out to my favorite noodle lady. Neither one of us knew each other's language, but we understood the need and desire to connect! She would serve me the best $1 pho; anyone could ever ask for! We would tell each other stories, and obviously just go by body motion and physical touch for emphasis. She reminded me of both of my Grandmothers, who always loved to cook and tell stories! I often wonder what happened to that sweet old lady, if she is still on that street corner, and I wish I could tell her that she left a monumental impression on me and I'll always have fond memories of Vietnam due to her.

One of my friends flew to Hanoi, Vietnam to visit me and we went to Sapa and Halong Bay, which were 4–5-hour bus rides away from Hanoi. Sapa was known for the expansive rice fields, hiking, and natural beauty. Sapa was uniquely beautiful, but those rice fields were very tricky, and they all started to look alike. One day when my friend and I were walking along the rice fields and we seemed to have become lost, some ladies appeared out of nowhere. We didn't know each other's language, but they started to guide us along the right path. Now mind you, I told my friend that we would end having to tip them but neither one of us brought money. After a couple of hours, they led us to their village and started holding their hands out, we started (fastly) walking away and apologizing. We followed the road for another mile or two and finally found our homestay right as it was getting dark. We started laughing because of the sheer luck we had had, because we would have easily been sleeping on one of those rice fields that night.

We enjoyed the scenery of the Sapa, but we couldn't wait to see what Halong Bay was about! On May 8, 2016 as we made our way to Halong Bay, we noticed that our phones weren't working properly, and the tour guide told us to not worry but the internet connection probably got turned off due to protests that were happening all over Vietnam due to environmental issues. I was intrigued because in that moment I remembered that I was in a Communist country and they can and will control the media and internet if they see fit. Mind you, the protests were peaceful and concerned the overfishing of certain areas in Vietnam. It was a reminder that I took certain liberties for granted. Could you imagine if the U.S. government shut off internet communications? People would go to the streets with weapons and demand access! As I was thinking about this, I put it to the side so that I could focus on the adventure ahead! The word Ha Long means "descending dragon" and this is a UNESCO World Heritage Site, so it is protected by the government. Once we got to our cruise ship and set our belongings down, we started looking around and were excited by the prospect of what we were going to see on this two-night cruise. My friend and I got to lay out in the sun, go on a hike to some caves and then take a kayak to a small watering hole where we got to swim. I have an irrational fear of kayaks because of the notion of my legs being trapped if the boat flips. Of course, what happens? The boat flipped and I struggled to get my legs out of the kayak. When I finally did, I saw everyone laughing, and I was so mad but what happened happened and I can't change it, glad I had put my swimsuit on. Halong Bay was a gorgeous sight to see and when visiting northern Vietnam, it is a must do! When it came time for us to return to Hanoi for our flight to Da Nang, I was sad, but the show must go on!

We had one day in Hanoi before our flight to Da Nang, which was great because I had to go to the hospital again. I got severely sunburnt between the hikes in Sapa and laying out on the cruise ship in Halong Bay. This hospital experience was so different, I went to an expat hospital, and was told to sit down and wait because they had to call a dermatologist to come in and see me. I felt special, and when the doctor came, she looked at my skin and chuckled. She prescribed me some lotion with steroids in it and told me to get a strong sunblock for my future travels. At least I could walk out of that hospital without using a crutch! Thankfully, I was seen that night, as we left for Da Nang the next day.

Da Nang is known for beautiful beaches, and better yet the gateway to Hoi An! Hoi An is a peaceful and quaint city, which used to be a port city, so it has indigenous and foreign influences. As we strolled along the main street in Hoi An, we saw tailor shops, restaurants, and gift shops. We saw this cute sign for a restaurant called the *Secret Garden* and we decided to give it a try! It was down an alleyway, which gave it some mystery and allure. When we walked down the alley and it opened into this beautiful, serene garden area with a pond on the side of the sit-down dining area. It was truly magical.

What else was so special was the fact that the owner ran a scholarship foundation for Vietnamese boys and girls who were struggling to get into university. I sponsored a Vietnamese boy whose mother had died, and the father was unable to work due to a motorbike accident. It was the equivalent of $400 but it would help him graduate high school and apply to university, which blew my mind because school fees cost way more in the United States. I was able to spread my Dad's legacy overseas and help someone achieve their dreams. The look of appreciation from the boy was so fulfilling, and it made me so proud. It was a great way to end our stay in Hoi An. Leaving Hoi An was hard, but I couldn't wait to go down south and explore Ho Chi Minh City. I decided to be adventurous and cheap, and I took a 24-hour bus ride between Ho Chi Minh City. I don't think I will ever be that cheap ever again. I was cramped on a sleeper bus with complete strangers, and I would nod off to sleep, but then jerk awake to make sure no one was watching me or trying to take my money or passport. I really would do random crazy things, but I figured I only had one life to live so go for it! What's the worst that could happen?

Usually I was the oldest tourist (yeah 30 was "old") in the room at my hostel, and I would sit and watch people and wonder how they could miss out on beautiful sunrises and early museum entrances. Learning about world history in whatever country you happen to be visiting is so special. After going to countries like Cambodia and Vietnam where war had devastated them and continues to linger, it's always interesting to see how a country can rise above their circumstances. I go to museums and I'm just astonished as to why this devastation was not in our history books growing up, we only get one side to the story. Which is why it is so important to get out and travel and see other perspectives and ways of living.

I found myself in Ho Chi Minh and wanted to learn more about the history of the Vietnam War, so of course I headed out to a museum in the early morning. As I'm perusing the artifacts and knowledge boards, I hear a young French girl ask her mother, "Why did the Americans do this to Vietnam?" and the mother's reply has always stuck with me, she said, "Because Americans love to take what is not theirs and hurt people in the process". I was stunned! The mother saw me look at her and she just nodded at me and seemed for me to agree with her now whether she suspected me to be American or African, I'm not sure. Throughout my journey in Asia, I was often mistaken for being African, but more on that later. That woman's response to her daughter got me thinking ... What does the rest of the world think about Americans?

I know our history of pillaging, plundering, and slavery takes our country what the blood stains it has left behind cyclone; but what does the average person think? When I was on a tour in Ho Chi Minh city, I decided to ask the tour director about how Vietnamese people view Americans in the present day. He said that for the most part the Vietnamese people love Americans, especially President Obama. President Barack Obama was in office at the time, why don't you know that while I was in Ho Chi Minh city he was in Hanoi! I had missed him by a day or two! He just sat in someone's noodle shop and ate with locals! Anyways back to the Ho Chi Minh tour ... I went to the Ho Chi Minh tunnels, which were made by the Viet Cong, who wanted to bring down the United States from the inside.

Those tunnels were crazy small! I tried going down one hole and couldn't go past my hips. My tour guide explained to me that these tunnels were one of the major reasons the United States lost the war. He described and showed us where the Viet Cong could pop up and steal supplies, food, and beer from the US campsites. I asked my tour guide why the Viet Cong didn't just kill the US troops since they could pop up on them at any time? He mentioned it was not their intent to kill troops unless they HAD to. I took it as if you poke and prod a bear too much, eventually it will lash out and kill you! These were people who wanted to be left alone! The Vietnamese people were first controlled by China for over 1000 years, then the French for 100 years, then US troops were in Vietnam for about 20 years. The Vietnamese were obviously tired of other countries placing a stronghold on them! I remember the narrative taught to me as a kid, that the Vietnamese were evil and full of hatred towards Americans, how ridiculous!

With my newfound knowledge, I returned to Hanoi so that I could volunteer at an English school. The younger generation of Vietnamese want to learn English to go to school and get better paying jobs anywhere throughout the world. I was shocked to see 2-to-80-year-olds in the classroom willing to learn English! The man that ran the school, Paul, did so for free! I was able to teach there and stay at his house with other teachers for free room and board.

Talking to Paul, I realized that he has close ties to Vietnam. He fought in the Vietnam/American war. He always mentioned the death and devastation that was caused by America and specifically him. When he returned home after the war, he said he built a life, but it wasn't the best because of everything he went through during the war. At age 50, he sold everything and moved to Vietnam to right his wrongs. Paul said if the American government won't do it, I'll try to give back in the best possible way. Therefore, his free English school started! I wanted to figure out what my legacy was going to be. For Paul it was his free English school to give back to a country that he took from! It got me thinking about what talents and skills I had and how I could use them to better society.

When it was time for me to leave Vietnam, I was sad, I literally cried from Paul's house all the way to the airport. I remember the taxi driver in his broken English asking me if he did something wrong. I replied to him, "No Sir you are fine", and I gave him the thumbs up. I said, "I am incredibly sad to leave your country. I love your country". I'm not sure if the taxi driver understood me or not but he nodded in agreement and drove me to the airport. I remember boarding my flight from Vietnam to Laos and still being in tears. As I look back on that moment, I know Vietnam is one of my favorite countries I've been to, but I believe I was also sad and in tears because I still at this time did not know what I wanted my purpose to be in life. I feel like I was getting close, but I still was not there. I was not at the finish line.

# CHAPTER 19:

## "*Scream*"

-Michael Jackson and Janet Jackson

I remember when I was in Southeast Asia, and I wanted a new experience after about four months of being there. I felt like I had grown comfortable, and I wanted to spice it up a bit. I knew I had to be in Croatia to meet a friend on a specific date and I had booked about 10 days in Egypt before going to Croatia, since I was going to go to Egypt by myself. I had traveled solo all this time, except when family or friends wanted to meet up with me, but I ended up booking a guided tour for Egypt because my family members and Troy were extremely uneasy about me going there by myself. This fear stemmed from what the media shows on TV, you know the bombings and shootings in tourist areas and the social unrest in Egypt, so I booked a guided tour. That eased their worry a bit so that they wouldn't feel so bad, so I had about two weeks free to be where I wanted and do what I wanted to do, before having to be in Egypt.

I remembered talking to an Indian American couple back in Vietnam at Paul's free English school about India. I don't know but for some odd reason, I thought it would be cool to go to India at that moment. India was never on my travel horizon nor was there ever an urge to go there, other than wanting to visit the Taj Mahal. Seeing one of the Seven World Wonders and to check it off my bucket list was a big factor in this determination to go to India. I remember when I told my Mom and Troy about my thoughts of going to India, they both said "but what will you eat? You don't like Indian food!" and they definitely had a point there! I had only tried Indian food once prior and what I ate didn't agree with me, so I never tried it again. I realized if I was serious about visiting India, I was going to have to suck it up and figure it out!

The Indian American couple kept telling me so much about India, and the side of India that the media doesn't show you (of course) and it had me intrigued to find out more. This couple was super accommodating and helpful with telling me places to see and what to look out for if I ever go. The couple was from Kerala, India which is the southern part of the country, but Taj Mahal is in the northern part and a part of, what many travelers call the Golden Triangle, which is a circuit between the cities of New Delhi, Agra (where the Taj Mahal is), and Jaipur. When I told them that I was seriously thinking about going to India, they immediately wanted to help and asked their cousin who lives in New Delhi if I could use his apartment as base for my Indian travels. He obliged and so I booked a one-way ticket out of Thailand to New Delhi, India.

Little did I know what I was going to be greeted with when I landed. As soon as I landed, went through customs to grab my bags, and headed out to find a reputable taxi company...I was bombarded! ALL my senses were tingling! Smell was attacked first, it smelled like exhaust fumes mixed with lots of manure and sweat; the smell seemed to have leaked into my taste buds as I stood in the airport lobby area looking at taxi companies. Then it seemed as if my sight was infiltrated with the smell because as I looked around to find where the smell was coming from, it was coming from all around me! There was no specific point that it started. Don't get me started on the deafening noises that you can hear as well. People shouting, horns honking, something that sounds like a crash every few minutes. I mean the cars, tuk tuks, and buses were bumper to bumper, so a crash wouldn't be a surprise. Final sense that was assaulted was touch. As I am looking around for a reputable taxi company that *Lonely Planet* suggested, some man grabbed my elbow and motioned for me to follow him. I yelled out, "DO NOT TOUCH ME!" and he let go. I try not to look the part of a tourist, but I know in that moment I probably had a neon sign pointing at my head that read "TOURIST COME TAKE ADVANTAGE OF ME!".

Once I negotiated a reasonable price with a taxi driver, we headed off to the cousin's residence. For some reason I was more aware of myself in this moment than I had been in a while, but didn't I ask for this? Now I felt myself stressing out due to the decision of coming to India. I kept looking out the window and asking myself, where are you and what have you done? I kept seeing deranged and skinny looking cows, goats, and random other farm animals roaming the street, piles of trash like so much trash that no one knew where to take it or do with it, and the overwhelming sense of distaste and smell. I legit felt like Dorothy in Oz, scared but intrigued at the same time.

Once we pull up to the area of my friend's cousin's house and I climb up the stairs to his apartment, I start to get excited. Like girl! You made it to India! The cousin greets me at the door and immediately shows me around then asks if I'm hungry. Right after he asked, my stomach made a noise in favor of this question so he asked what I would like. I told him that I didn't know what to order because the previous time I tried Indian food; I didn't like it. He told me not to worry and that he would be able to figure out what I like. He ended up ordering chicken biryani and it was DELICIOUS! He was so pleased and glad that I wouldn't totally starve in India.

The next day, I go out for a little adventure and as I'm walking around on the New Delhi streets, I realize I'm getting stared at which is not totally out of the norm for me, but the men's eyes would linger. I thought to myself...I'm totally covered, what could they be looking at other than my black skin? I decided to pack that moment away in my brain for the moment, because my stomach started to rumble so it meant it was time to feed it. I happened to come upon a sandwich shoppe and decided to order, now I have no idea what I ordered, and I prayed that it would come out edible. Thankfully, it was good! I went back to their cousin's place and began preparation to go to Jaipur which is a part of the Golden Triangle travel loop that tourists like to do.

When I arrived in Jaipur, it was a bit cleaner than New Delhi but still busy and loud. I got to my hostel room and set my things down and by the time my phone got charged up, I remember trying to leave around 8pm to get some food because I hadn't eaten due to traveling. The hostel worker blocked my way from leaving and he asked me where I was going, I told him that I was going to get food. He proceeded to beg me to not leave the hostel this late and he could call and have food delivered for me. I was like what could be that bad that I can't walk down the street to get my own food at 8pm? I had no idea that it would be a bad idea (as a woman) to leave when it was dark. By the time I got my food delivered and went back to my hostel room, I was too tired to even be mad or figure out what to feel.

The next day a few new girls came into the hostel room, so I introduced myself to two Canadians who were in the same room and we instantly got along with each other. We decided to go out to buy saris and have dinner together and I remember walking along the street, because you just walk anywhere and everywhere there's space, and I hear one of the girls yell out and then I see this Indian man running away and laughing. The girl had gotten her butt slapped by that man and I'm so glad it wasn't me; I probably would've run after him and beat him so bad that I would've ended up in an Indian prison. Who wants that? These situations made me remember that first moment when I noticed how much attention I was receiving from men in the country. Made me be more aware of my surroundings.

One day, I was out in the street market looking at different trinkets and shoes to go with my sari and I guess I lost track of time because the sun was starting to set, and I knew that wasn't good. All the sudden, loud shouting caught my attention and when I looked out at the street, I saw about a dozen men screaming and yelling. I have no idea what about, but I knew at that moment it was time to go. Once I got my items paid for, the crowd of men had grown about double in size. I'm looking around and of course, with my luck, I see no other women. I immediately thought to myself, why do I put myself in these types of predicaments? As I was lamenting myself, I heard a man shout "MISS MISS, come here!" and I looked at the crowd of shouting men which had grown to about 30 at this time and I looked at the shopkeeper and decided I could handle one versus 30.

When I stepped into the shop, he showed me around and he sold jewelry, purses, and belts. He mentioned how it was extremely dangerous for me to be out there by myself especially when so many drunk Indian men were fighting. I asked him what they were fighting about, and he said alcohol. Apparently only so much alcohol was served by a specific time and after that, they were left up to their own devices which meant sometimes they took to the streets. I'm not going to lie; I was grateful that this man saw me and called for me to come into his shop. I had told him what had happened to those girls in the market, and he then told me that he would escort me around Jaipur. At first, I was like well I don't know you either, but my intuition also told me that I could trust him.

After the crowd dissipated, he walked me back to my hostel and thank goodness because it was pitch black by now. I thanked him and he told me to come by his shop the next morning and he would slowly escort me around Jaipur. The next day I went to his shop and he told me to have a seat because he had just ordered chicken biryani, I was so excited! When it got delivered, he grabbed a stack of newspapers and started to place everything on top of them... no plates, no silverware, not even a napkin. I put some hand sanitizer on my hands and prayed over my food then literally dug in! Eating with my hands and using the naan bread, really reminded me of my time in SE Asia where I had to get comfortable with eating with chopsticks. Totally out of my comfort zone, but I had to eat!

When we were done eating, we hopped on his motorbike and headed to a fabric and leather factory. I had never seen such beautiful colors and I had a pink, orange, blue, and yellow sari made with satin material. I knew I would be headed to Agra soon, and I wanted to wear a sari to the Taj Mahal. My personal escort was taking me to see the most beautiful parts of Jaipur, but there were also some devastating portions. Some of the living conditions were so poor, that Skid Row in LA would've felt luxurious. Some of these people had only cardboard, plastic, and dirt to use. I tried not to stare, but I had never seen anything like it. The only thing that came close was the favelas in Brazil, and at least those slums came with mostly solid roofs over their heads. It was another moment where I was thankful for what I had in life because it can always be worse. Riding on the back of the motorbike was exhilarating and insightful but I couldn't wait to move onto the city of Agra, where the Taj Mahal is.

The next day, I caught a four-hour train ride with the

two Canadian girls I met in Jaipur. We were all so excited and couldn't wait to see the glorious Taj Mahal! As we pulled into Agra, I noticed how flooded with water and how much litter and trash was stacked in huge piles. Plus, the combination of those two, made the smell so much worse than what I smelled in New Delhi. So many kids run alongside the train tracks to greet each train, which I thought was cute, but I wondered how they could navigate around the huge piles of discarded junk. Furthermore, I wondered why their government doesn't do a better job about cleaning and preserving their land. I had assumed, that because this magnificent world wonder was in this city, that Agra would be pristine. Obviously, I was wrong.

When we got a taxi to take us from the train station to our hostel, we drove past the Taj Mahal and got to see it from a distance. The taxi driver explained to us that the Taj Mahal was built by an emperor for his deceased wife, who died during childbirth. He loved this woman so much that he commissioned this palace to be made in her honor and memory. It is a love story that could make any girl swoon and become mesmerized by the majestic beauty and, in that moment, it made me think of Troy. Would he ever pay ode to me if I died before him? Does he love me that much? I wondered if we would get married, although we've discussed it in the past, it wasn't anything that I pressured him about especially because look at me! I'm halfway across the world, how could I make him settle down, when I'm not in the same country as him and I'm still trying to figure out how I fit into this big world!

The girls and I woke up before dawn the next day because we were told to get to the Taj Mahal entrance before sunrise so we can get there before most of the other tourists. I remember tying my sari up, the best way I could remember to and asking the girls for help. I took one look at myself in the mirror and my hair. My afro was looking nice and moisturized, and it was BIG! Little did I know what I was going to walk into that morning.

The entrance to the Taj Mahal was nothing short of amazing. Even before reaching the front gates, you will notice a visible change in how pristine the area looks, like there's a special cleaning crew just for the Taj Mahal grounds. When our crew took all the necessary pictures at the gate and captured the Taj Mahal, we started to move more into the garden space so we could take more pictures. The Taj Mahal is so grand and so gorgeous, it almost felt out of place amongst its surroundings. It was being refurbished while we were there, but it was majestic, and you could tell that so much love went into this structure. It is really a shame that the emperor's wife never got to see it! I was so excited to finally be in the presence of this world wonder and be in my traditional sari! As we got closer and closer to the actual palace, I started seeing a lot of older Indian women looking at me and pointing. I instantly thought "uh oh what did I do now?". At first, a handful of these women came over to me and cornered me and started looking at my sari and hair. I started to understand at that moment what was about to transpire.

Like I mentioned before, I tried my best to tie my sari the traditional way but apparently, I didn't do a great job because these women started helping me fix it. I also noticed that women were wanting to touch my hair and then take pictures with me. It was cute at first, but then as more people saw me taking pictures, they started coming towards me. It got to be too much, I eventually had to leave that corner and do a fast-paced walk to get away! I know that I was probably the first black woman they had seen in person and they were amazed, but I also have personal boundaries. I was learning to vocalize when those boundaries were getting crossed, but a part of me still felt bad. I didn't want them to think negatively of me, let alone the whole race. Seems silly to most, but at times throughout my travels in Asia, I felt like I had to carry that on my shoulders especially knowing that you are maybe the first black woman or person they've ever seen! You don't want to ruin it for the next ones to come along!

Later that afternoon at the Agra Red Fort I was met with the same points and stares. The Agra Red Fort felt like a city within a city, it was more so a palace than a regular fort. Almost like the Taj Mahal it was built and rebuilt for one of the emperor's favorite empresses. The walls of the entrance were so tall and huge that it was a bit intimidating. The girls and I had to walk away because of how many people wanted to take a picture of us. It almost felt like we were art exhibits. I walked to the outskirts of the entrance of the fort and sat down to rest and wouldn't you know, a woman put their baby in my arms and positioned their children around me to take a picture. I was mortified because I realized that a line had started to form. I didn't want to be anyone's zoo exhibit anymore. I started forcibly saying no and got up to walk away. Thankfully, the rest of our group was ready to leave, and we all walked out together. I just know my picture is on some random Indian mantels or wherever they hang their treasured photos.

After leaving Agra, I returned to Jaipur for a couple days and then headed back to New Delhi. Have you ever heard of the term Delhi belly? I ventured down the street and stopped at a local kitchen for chicken biryani, because I've soon realized that's my "main Indian dish". Well once I ordered it, I peeked at the actual kitchen since it was somewhat open, and I intuitively knew I would be in trouble. The floors of the kitchen looked black and sticky, and I saw a cockroach or two. I figured well maybe that means this will be the best biryani, I'll ever eat! I had already spent my money and I didn't want to waste it, so I took my chances. Prayed over my food and hoped for the best.

It was DELICIOUS, but within a couple hours I came to regret my adventurous decision. My stomach started making loud and discouraging sounds and the pain that followed...it knocked the wind out of my lungs. I have had stomach aches in the past, but this was something out of this world. Every time I moved, I thought I was going to throw up or poop on myself. Lucky me, getting sick in an area that frowns upon flushing toilet paper, if you can even find some of that! I would usually carry extra toilet paper with me, so luckily, I had some and as I was sitting on the toilet for like the 9th time, I remembered that I had a prescription for Ciprofloxacin or Cipro for short. In my research before leaving America, I realized that I just may need some, so I had my doctor prescribe them for me. I didn't think I would have to use them until Egypt, but there I was, a few days before going to Egypt and starting to pop these pills like they were candy.

I called my Mom and Troy to send them my last wishes, as I thought I was getting eaten up from the inside out. Both my Mom and Troy were not fazed by my dramatics and asked me if I was going to be well enough in 24 hours to get on my flight to Turkey. I told them yes, because I'm going to carry out my travels so they said to rest and stop crying so I can save my energy. Sometimes you just need that type of tough love. Despite everything that transpired, I was so grateful to have had time in India and experience this culture for about two weeks. I know there is more to see, and I would go back to explore, if the opportunity presented itself. India gave me so many tools to use on future travels, and I highly suggest everyone to go and see this mysterious yet majestic country for yourself!

# CHAPTER 20:

## "Remember The Time"

-Michael Jackson

I was so excited for my next destination because it was another country that I thought I was never going to get to see, but here I was getting ready to go to Turkey! It was July 15, 2016, I will never forget when I was in the New Delhi airport, gathering my things up and heading to check in for my flight to Istanbul and something on the television monitors caught my eyes. I saw tanks rolling through a city, but I didn't think much of it until I saw panicked looks on other people's faces. I set my backpack down and looked closer at the screen, the tanks were rolling through the city of ISTANBUL! I didn't quite understand who was disagreeing with who, but I knew I couldn't go to Turkey that day. As I stood there in shock, with my mouth wide open, I started wondering what I should do next. I was set to depart from New Delhi to Istanbul within a couple hours! Interestingly enough, I didn't freak out. I just walked over to the ticket agent and pointed to the screen and asked what could I do? I told him that I had to be in Cairo by a certain date and I was using Istanbul as a 48-hour layover, so the ticket agent changed my ticket to go straight to Cairo on July 15th instead of July 17th, which was my Dad's birthday. He and I always talked about Egyptian culture when I was a kid.

I was very saddened that this situation occurred, when I was on that side of the world and finally had some time to venture to Turkey, but safety comes first. Also, they shut down multiple airports in Turkey due to the military coup, so I couldn't fly in anyways! As I waited for my flight to Cairo, I had some time to look up what was going on in Turkey. I knew it was on the "list" that Americans should be aware of going to, but I barely paid any attention to that (and still don't), call me crazy or adventurous! For me, it is extremely hard to understand what goes on in war torn countries and which media outlets to believe, especially when my own country sticks their hands into the pot and stirs it up. Like many countries in the Middle East, the United States will support whichever leader they deem worthy of protecting our interests at that time, not necessarily the specific country's interest. Throughout my travels, I have seen this time and time again...Vietnam, Cambodia, and Egypt to name a few. My country is not horrible, but it has set a precedent for appearing to need and want world dominion in any means necessary. Which is why I think it is so necessary for Americans to go and explore other cultures and countries and celebrate our differences, those differences are beautiful. I don't wish to travel to mark off a country on my "been there, done that" list, but to truly learn from another's perspective. There are always multiple sides to the same story, and I don't mind hearing each one. You may gain a new perspective and understanding, and even better...a new friend!

Even though I did not get to reach Turkey, I am grateful that I got to have this experience of growth. Had this happened to me earlier in my travels, I probably would've had a complete meltdown, but I took this setback in stride and stood my ground and made another way. Solo travel can profoundly change you and make you realize you had strength that you didn't know was there! As I moved through certain countries and situations, I was found I was gaining building blocks of a stronger foundation than when I started my trip. Those were the moments I had hoped for because when I started this journey, I wasn't sure where it would lead. I wasn't sure where it would lead me country wise AND mentally, emotionally, and spiritually. I probably should've given myself a pat on the back for how I handled that Turkey situation, but there was no time for that! I was heading to Egypt!

Egypt had always been on my bucket list of countries to go to. Even as a little girl being so enamored with the culture and the movies about Egypt, I just couldn't get enough of them. Even though it is not historically sound, *The Mummy* is one of my all-time favorite movies. I know it's cheesy, but it made me want to go to Egypt even more. As a young girl, I would watch Michael Jackson's music video for "Remember the Time" over and over! It featured Eddie Murphy as the Pharaoh and Iman as the Queen, and of course Michael Jackson had the Queen fall in love with him through his song and dancing. I always pictured myself as that Queen that would seek adventure over a boring man in power. Egypt being in Africa and the Pharaohs, all of it interested me and I couldn't wait to go! Since I was already going to be traveling throughout the world, I figured why not stop in Egypt? When I was told my family that I wanted to go to Egypt, they were very uneasy about it because of all of what the media shows of the violence and political unrest. I was so determined to go there, so I made a compromise and l booked a guided tour. That calmed the tension down a bit. I was still ill as I was leaving India and going to Cairo, Egypt, so thankfully, there was a guide to pick me up from the airport that helped navigate the Egyptian visa process. It was interesting, because had he not been there, I may have had an issue getting in, which was my first indication of tension between the US and Egypt. When the customs person looked at my passport, she shook her head, and grimaced. The tour guide spoke to her, and I'm assuming he told her that I'm on a tour and this is legit, because she finally and begrudgingly stamped my passport.

As the tour guide took the hotel where the whole tour was going to kick off, we drove past some of the pyramids, and I was just thrilled. I was ecstatic and speechless. I couldn't put into words, what this moment felt like for someone who had desired to come to this country for so long. When I got to the hotel, I was told that there would be a welcome dinner at six o'clock. And I decided to lay down because of how tired I was from being ill and traveling. I slept through the welcome dinner, which was okay, because I don't think I would have been able to eat anyways. But the very next day, I got to meet with the tour. And we all were so excited to be there. There was one other American that was on the tour, as well, so of course we bonded. It was fun to meet everybody from all over the world in our little tour group, there were people from New Zealand, Australia, Great Britain, and Colombia. It was amazing for all these different cultures and countries to come together in one tour group. Our tour guide mentioned that he was so happy that we chose to visit Egypt despite how our respective media may portray it. He also mentioned that it was a great idea for tourists to book an escorted tour, not only for safety but also so that you know what you're looking at and can learn! At certain points in the tour, we did have an armed guard escort us between specific cities due to unrest. It was a little weird at first, but we ended up getting used to it. It was interesting to be there in that time of unrest, but nothing happened.

I remember going on a hot air balloon ride over the pyramids, and just being able to look down at all the pyramids, palm trees, and sand and just realizing how blessed I was in that moment. Not only was I finally in Egypt, but I was checking off another bucket list item which was being in a hot air balloon. Passing by pyramids that were built thousands of years ago and just thanking God at being given the chance to be here and witness that. We got to go into the different tombs of Pharaohs past and we could envision the lap of luxury that they had. I was looking at sand and stone, but I could picture gold and white stone and ornate drippings around the palace with the Pharaoh and his Queen sitting on majestic thrones. I was not naive to know that slaves Pharaohs had built their luxurious surroundings. I equated it to what happened in America, the colonizers had to build the luxurious surroundings using slaves as well. It made me wonder even more why one race or culture thinks that they can enslave another one? I don't know if I will ever know the answer to that, but it was an extra special treat to go see a Nubian village.

Visiting a Nubian village was special to me, especially after my tour guide called them barbaric at one point when I asked why the Greek colonizers didn't want to go further south beyond Egypt at first. He replied, "they didn't want to go into the jungles and deal with the barbaric people". That also boggled my mind, as Egypt is IN AFRICA, but they consider themselves Middle Eastern. Also, the fact that the Nubians were the first to build pyramids and then Greeks/Egyptians saw that and wanted it for themselves. To this day, I'm not sure how widespread that information is but the South Sudanese pyramids were built first. That is something that a historian must unpack and I'm not on that level by far. Nubians were from what we call South Sudan today, and they had darker skin. It was very fascinating and interesting as we walked through the Nubian village. On the guided tour, I'm the only African American in the group, so when we entered the Nubian village, the villagers started shouting at me, "Queen, Queen, come, come, look! Our African goddess, please come look!" And I'm just basking in all those accolades because in America, you don't get called a Queen or an African goddess. Those choice words usually aren't the ones that come to people's minds when they think of black women. So, I was drinking all this attention in and I got asked to help prepare food, which even my tour guide thought was unique. Even with the limited amount of English that the ladies knew, we were able to communicate, through head nods, pointing, and laughter. I felt so grateful in that moment to be able to help prepare our meal and see how they live. I was honored to be a part of that moment where I was able to be with those women and talk with them, even if they didn't understand me completely. It was another example of how a smile and laughter can go a long way, and it was one of the greatest moments of my Egyptian trip. Being here made me think about my ancestry, and it made me want to dive deeper, because who knows, I could be related to Queen Nefertiti!

Our tour group was interviewed by a local Cairo news station about promoting tourism for Cairo and Egypt as a whole. We let the people know how safe we felt and that you should book a guided tour if possible. At that moment, I realized how much tourism really means to Egyptian economy, and how it may be tied to the reason why there was so much violence at times. When people don't have resources, they turn to violence at times, it doesn't make it right, but I could see the correlation. I remember telling Troy and my family about my thoughts surrounding Egypt and how I felt like it was making me stronger, and it made me look at my surroundings in a deeper way. Not to just take the media's point of view on culture in countries but formulate my own opinion and voice it when necessary, and it was interesting to be able to tie that strength in finding my voice while working through the grief of losing my father.

It all tied together, and I didn't realize it at that point. I just thought I was having a great time, but it was so much deeper than that.

My Dad being a huge history buff would've been so fascinated by all the history in Egypt, or anywhere by the Nile River for that matter. I felt a special kind of energy there, like a new growth which would make sense; it was where the first civilization was birthed! Even though my Dad was apprehensive about getting his passport and traveling abroad, I know he would've loved this experience! He always told my brother and I that we were descendants of Kings and Queens, both Earthly AND Heavenly! So, keep our heads up, we can't get anything done in this world with our heads hanging low. My parents encouraged us to keep our heads held high as if a crown sits upon it.

# CHAPTER 21:

## *"Soon As I Get Home"*

-Faith Evans

After leaving Egypt, I went through different parts of Europe, both western and eastern, but I loved Eastern Europe! The prices were cheaper, the people were nicer, and beaches were so pristine and untouched! When I was at a beach restaurant on the island of Cyprus, I met an older lady and we swapped travel stories and laughed so much. Turned out that she owned the restaurant and ended up giving me my meal for free and as I sat there looking at the waves crash against the sand, I honestly couldn't believe that I ended up here. That I ended up taking this spectacular journey across the world, alone, and knowing that my time was ending made me both sad and nervous. I was sad because I love traveling, meeting new people, hearing different perspectives, but also nervous because I wasn't sure how Troy would react to the "new" me! I had gained so much knowledge about different cultures and myself, I had lost about 40 pounds, wearing my kinky curls loud and proud, I loved showing off my skin, because my black is beautiful! But even more so, my boldness and strength shined through more than it ever had in the past! That was one of the best lessons that traveling the world solo has taught me, is how to be strong.

I remember the flight home and how overwhelming it was. I wasn't sure how I was going to feel, how Troy was going to react. I had felt changed, but I didn't know how that change was going to affect my relationship with Troy. I wasn't sure if he was going to understand that I will never stop traveling. Was he going to understand that I was going to travel at any chance I could get? I'll never want to stop exploring the world because of what the world has taught me, so I was a bit apprehensive about returning home for that reason. I made sure that the flight attendants never left my wine glass empty, I was NERVOUS! I would listen to music and drift off to sleep, but then I would think of all the "what ifs" and wake up, I even thought to myself, "maybe I should've stayed". I was so scared that Troy wouldn't understand my insatiable thirst, that the world would beckon me, and I would answer that call, in a moment's notice. I don't think the word distraught even describes the anxiety I had during that plane ride, but once I landed in the United States, I knew it was time to prepare myself. Prepare to see Troy for the first time in almost nine months!

When I saw Troy standing in the airport to pick me up, I was ecstatic! All the worry and anxiety disappeared when I looked at his face, and I melted into our first hug after all that time away. I should have had more faith in Troy, because he may not have the same insatiable travel lust, but he understands that the woman that he fell in love with also has a love and passion for travel. Why would he try to take away something that gives me so much joy? Something that puts a smile on my face, which he loves that smile so much. Why would he want that part of me that he fell in love with to go away? That's why I love Troy because he allows the space for me to be me. And he loves me through and through! No matter where I go, he will be with me in my heart.

# CHAPTER 22:

## *"This Will Be"*

### -Natalie Cole

I was so excited to go to Disneyworld with Troy for New Year's Eve, especially because I felt like we needed special time for ourselves after I had been gone for nine months. Troy knew that Disneyworld has always been my happy place! I would tell him about going there as a kid with my family and he thought that was so neat. I loved going to Disney as a kid with my family, I remember those experiences more than I remember "things". My parents always told us to be thankful for the trips to Disneyworld, because not everyone gets to go. Of course, when I was 10 years old, I didn't understand that. Troy had never been as a kid, his first time going was with me at the age of 34. Even though Troy might not admit it, he loved it as much as I did. For these reasons, Disneyworld will always have a special place in my heart and soul!

Obviously, I have established how much I love Disneyworld, BUT going there during the Christmas/ NYE holiday season is even more magical! The beautifully decorated Christmas trees, seeing Mickey and Minnie

Mouse in their Christmas outfits, all the Christmas lights and decorations throughout the park, and of course the famous Christmas Parade! Everything about that specific timing is so magical and adds to the love and passion I have for Disney.

That whole day Troy spoiled me, I truly felt like a Disney Princess! I had matching shirts made for us, that had Mickey and Minnie Mouse on them. His shirt said LO at the top and SOUL at the bottom with Mickie leaning in for a kiss, while mine said VE at the top and MATE at the bottom with Minnie leaning in for a kiss. The whole day people were congratulating us, and we kept saying "thanks but we're just dating". As a matter of fact, Disney had opened some new exhibits and I finally got to meet a real live Ariel (The Little Mermaid) ...I fangirled so hard, it was embarrassing! She even mentioned that it was nice to see a beautiful couple. After we left that exhibit, I noticed a text from my friend, and she jokingly mentioned that Troy should propose to me THAT night. I told her that was silly, and he wouldn't do that! When I told Troy what she had said, he laughed it off and we kept going about our day!

We had visited most of my favorite attractions during the day, except for the Haunted Mansion. The Haunted Mansion was one of my Dad's favorite attractions to ride at Disney, so every time I go there, I must ride it! It was getting close to 8pm and Troy kept insisting that we be by Cinderella's castle before 9pm for the closing firework and light show. I wasn't sure what all the fuss was about since we've seen the fireworks numerous times. I begged him to just be carefree and not to worry about a specific time. Of course, he obliged and said let's ride the Haunted Mansion one more time before the fireworks. He knew that ride had and still has a great significance to me.

After we rode it, we made our way to the beautiful and majestic Cinderella castle to get a good spot for the fireworks. I remember we were sitting on a circular concrete fixture next to other couples and families. We were talking about dinner plans and what we should do the next day. The conversation shifted to what we wanted to do with our lives and chasing different dreams. We talked about these types of things often, especially with my experience with my Dad. I am a firm believer of living your life to the fullest. I was listening to Troy speak, but the distinct smell of popcorn caught my attention and I turned away from Troy. I remember asking him if he saw a popcorn stand and when I didn't get a response, I saw that he was halfway kneeling and holding a ring in his fingers. He was smiling and asked if we could chase our dreams together, forever.

I was so surprised, because I thought I would've been able to tell when Troy was going to propose. (I know I know...I have a bit of control freak tendencies.) Plus, when he asked me if we could continue to chase our dreams TOGETHER, I was left speechless! When I did finally recover from the shock, my first question was "Did you ask my Mom for her blessing or Paul?". Yeah, that is not what he wanted to hear in response. The only reason why I asked is because most of my life I spent pleasing others, especially my family. Even in that moment, I wanted their "permission" and all Troy wanted was ME! I had to remind myself of the soul-searching trip I took, and the adventurer I had become! I say yes to my future, no one else does!

After about 15 minutes of walking around, the closing fireworks show started. THAT is when something on the inside of me burst and the tears started flowing. I blame it on the Jiminy Cricket song, *"When You Wish Upon a Star"* playing plus the fireworks, the way Troy was watching me with both nauseating anticipation and unconditional love, and finally the way the rose gold, Princess cut diamond ring glistened in the night...how could I say no? The man knew me so well and how could I ever let him go? I FINALLY SAID YES!

# CHAPTER 23:

## *"Can You Stand The Rain"*

### -New Edition

For my 31st birthday, Troy and I went to New York City to celebrate. We stayed at my Uncle's bachelor pad in Manhattan and felt extra special because it was in the middle of almost everything we wanted to do and see. I had been to NYC multiple times, but this was Troy's first time, so it was special. My Uncle's place was near Central Park and I was excited because I had never been there before. Troy loves going to zoos, so it was only fitting that we went to the Central Park Zoo. We got to see all the normal zoo animals and we really were in awe at the fact of how big the zoo was, and even how big the park was! We didn't get to see the whole park, but I could see why people flock there and could stay there all day. It had an air of romance with the horse drawn carriages, but also a mysterious side to it with all the twists and turns and I wasn't sure where we may end up. Almost like my relationship with Troy, romantic but not knowing where life's twists and turns may end up.

In my never-ending randomness, one morning I talked Troy into taking the subway to Brooklyn for a special bagel shop that I had been drooling over on Instagram. It seemed like it took us forever to get to this bagel shop, but that's because I would daydream and make us miss our stop. Troy wasn't too happy with that, but he knew I didn't mean to do it on purpose. When we finally made it to the correct stop, Troy noticeably let out a sigh of relief and then we started walking the couple blocks it took to get to the bagel shop. Now, I'm not sure if you have been to NYC or not, but NYC's blocks are not normal blocks. Their blocks seem like it takes ten minutes to walk each block, so of course I didn't hear the end of how much walking it took to get to this bagel place. Troy obviously was not impressed so far with our little adventure. When we finally get to the bagel shop, we see how small it is! There is only space for about 4 people to sit down, so otherwise you are standing while ordering and then going outside to admire your bagel selection. I was so caught up in the moment with how glorious this place was and of course I had to get the unicorn colored one. It was multicolored and filled with funfetti cream cheese with all kinds of different colored sprinkles. Troy got a normal blueberry and plain cream cheese bagel, I was astonished! I couldn't believe after coming all this way, that is what he wanted to purchase. I was so happy, and I could tell that even though Troy wasn't that thrilled with the trek and how long it took to get here, he loved how much it made me smile. Troy often tells me that my smile is the reason why he fell in love with me and that he wants to keep that smile on my face for the rest of time if he can help it.

Later that day, we ended up going to visit the Statue of Liberty which is something else that I had never done as well. Troy kept complaining about having a headache, and I realized that he had been getting a lot of headaches recently, but we kept waving it off due to the injury he sustained at the factory job he had held during my world tour. A knot on his forehead had formed after the injury, so I told him that we would finally get it checked out after we got back home from NYC. We spent the rest of that day cruising along and seeing the Statue of Liberty from all angles and I remember Troy asked me how such an iconic statue that stood for liberty and freedom almost seemed to be a falsity because not everyone in the USA is free. During my world tour, I would tell him how certain countries were portrayed to be evil on our news media, but they weren't. Throughout my travels, I learned just how powerful and long the arm of the USA extends and how greedy our government can be. Remarkably interesting when you hear different sides to the same story when your shield is taken off. I remember Troy's parents were so concerned about me going to Vietnam because they thought that Vietnamese hated Americans due to the Vietnam War, which was so far from the truth. I know Troy's Dad had his various concerns due to him fighting in the Vietnam War, which I understood but I made sure he knew that I was fine and enjoying myself. As I mentioned previously, the Vietnamese love Americans and were overjoyed when President Obama was in office and made an appearance in their country. These types of conversations were important for us as an interracial couple, to have. We had to have this conversation in hushed tones because we didn't want to seem unpatriotic. I appreciate where I came from but being able to venture out and see all these beautiful countries, cultures, people, and food, it really changed my perspective on how I view the world. Literally. Even though Troy hadn't been out of the country, he really listened and digested the information that I shared with him. I could tell that his world was starting to change as he would see the world through my eyes but of course in actuality his (our) life was about to flip upside down.

# SECTION 3:
## Found

# CHAPTER 24:

## "Can't Give Up Now"

-Mary Mary

During our one and half hour (one way) trips to the Barrett Center at the University of Cincinnati hospital, we would put on our own mini car concerts. It was a way to destress and release some anxiety about the upcoming long treatment days. Some of our favorites were, Survivor's "Eye of the Tiger", anything by N'SYNC, Jagged Edge's "Let's Get Married", and Tupac's "Keep Ya Head Up", and as you can tell our musical genres cross all lines but also tell a story. I often use music to match my mood and energy, so on our drives down to Cincinnati we would be high energy and ready to take treatment by the horns and own it! Eventually Troy would fall asleep, and I would switch to Gospel, because as we got closer to the hospital, I would become more and more unraveled. Gospel always snaps me out of any kind of funk and reminds me that there's a reason why I'm here on earth. I just didn't know why at that point! Listening to Kirk Franklin, Mary Mary, and Lecrae really helped me personally prepare for our long day of treatments;

I needed a strength that I could rely on and nobody could steal.

On our drives home, the music would be more mellow at first so that I could get Troy comfortable. I would listen to gospel and then that would flow into Rick James, Chic, or KC and the Sunshine Band. Sometimes the toll of the whole day would start to creep up on me and have me so tired, that I would drift off to sleep while driving! I remembered an old trick that my Dad used to do, he would roll down the window and blast his music, so naturally I did the same thing! You see, my Grandpa Jackson (my Dad's Dad), fell asleep while driving his car, crashed, and died. My Dad was only about 8 or 9 years old when his Dad passed away and I was only about 25 years old when my Dad passed away. I was determined to NOT die early, so I did what I knew to do...roll down that window and blast Migos and Cardi B. Troy would then wake up with disgust from my musical choice, but I didn't care at that moment. I NEEDED that moment for myself!

# CHAPTER 25:

## "Looking For You"

### -Kirk Franklin

After celebrating my birthday in NYC, Troy had gotten such a bad headache that he went to Urgent Care. The doctors there mentioned that the knot on his forehead was more than likely a contusion and to put a cold compress on it and take Tylenol or Advil for the pain and until the swelling went down. I wasn't comfortable with their flippant "diagnosis", so I asked if they could refer Troy to an ENT (ear, nose, and throat) specialist since Troy had had some nasal issues when he was younger. They also referred him to a brain and head trauma specialist. Both doctors practiced within 15 minutes of us, and both wanted Troy to have an MRI of his head/neck area. Neither one of the doctors were sure what they were looking at, regarding Troy's MRI results, but the ENT specialist told us to either go to James Cancer Center in Columbus or U.C. Hospital in Cincinnati for a definite diagnosis because he believed that it could be a cancerous tumor. I was furious, how dare he insinuate that Troy could have cancer! I remember driving us back home and I dropped Troy off and I went to go see my Mom at her job, and I just melted into her arms as I told her what the doctor said. All the ladies at her job stopped what they were doing and came around us and started praying for Troy and me, and then my Mom said to schedule Troy's appointment asap for whichever hospital chain we felt led to going to.

Troy decided that he wanted to go see the ENT specialist in Cincinnati since he was already familiar with this doctor. Starting at the age of 17, Troy initially thought he had a stubborn booger that wouldn't come out, but once his nostril got blocked and he couldn't breathe well, he knew something was wrong. He was diagnosed with nasal polyps and was referred to this same doctor for his care. Troy had to have these benign polyps removed, but they kept coming back. He got these polyps due to secondhand smoke. *I just want to take this time and implore anyone and everyone, please stop smoking. If not for your own health, but those that live with you and love you.* I know Troy questions and wonders why and how he got those polyps but not his two brothers, just like I questioned why my Dad had to leave this Earth but here we are, and we must move forward.

Troy ended up having EIGHT surgeries over the course of four years to get all the nasal polyps out, which left him with no sense of smell. I can't even imagine losing any of my senses, let alone SMELL! All the wonderful senses that this world has to offer, like flowers, perfume, and food...he can only catch a whiff of gasoline and other strong scents. I know he misses the smell of bacon, cotton candy, and White Castle burgers (YUCK!) but he often buys me perfume and tells me that he wishes that he could smell it on me, and just smell ME! My heart crumbles whenever he says that because it is something that we all take for granted. Something so simple as smell, can have such a huge impact on life but we don't think about it.

Once he got through those eight surgeries, he was told that there was a slim chance (10% to be exact) that the polyps could come back as cancerous tumors. Troy was checked yearly for these polyps but stopped going after three years thinking that they would never come back. Which of course, led us to March 2017, when we are trying to see who can tell us what is going on with my fiancé! We told the same doctor that Troy had seen so many years ago, about his headaches and nosebleeds. They took more X-Rays and did another MRI and determined that they wanted to do a biopsy to see if the mass was a cancerous tumor. We were still hopeful that it wouldn't be cancer because of Troy's age and overall good health. The doctor even mentioned that IF it were cancer, they could probably easily go in and remove it like he did with the nasal polyps so many years ago. I'm trying to combat my dreadful feelings of despair and dread, but I remembered I had to be Troy's cheerleader. We didn't know anything for sure yet, so there was no reason to show fear especially when it would make Troy scared.

I'll never forget March 28, 2017, when Troy's scheduled appointment wasn't at his normal doctor's office but at the Barrett Cancer Center. I remember walking towards this Center and saying, "oh this can't be good" and Troy heard me and got quiet. As soon as I touched the door handle, I just had this sickening and sinking feeling in my heart. I just knew. That door felt heavy, almost too heavy for me to open and I wanted to turn around and run away. Sometimes, I wish that I would've grabbed Troy's hand and told him let's run away to a remote island, but we wouldn't be here, and you wouldn't be reading this story.

This Barrett Cancer Center looked small on the outside but as soon as you get through those doors, you clearly see just how big the inside is and how many floors there are. It was overwhelming, for so many different reasons. Why are we meeting at a CANCER center? Why are there so many people? Why does cancer hit this many families? What is next for my family that I'm trying to have? Troy and I checked in for his appointment and waited to be seen, which was excruciating! All the hurry up and wait, all the anticipation like we are about to see Beyoncé, and Jay-Z perform, but no, we are waiting in a hospital waiting to see what trajectory our life's path was about to take. Those 10-15 minutes seemed like it took forever! Caregivers you know what I'm talking about! I just want to be told what is happening and how to prepare my life around the news, but nothing could've prepared me for what I was about to hear.

When we got called back to see the Doctor, I remember firmly holding Troy's hand as a reassurance that I had his back. I'm not going anywhere. When the doctor came in, he explained that the biopsy did show that the nasal blockage was indeed cancer. Troy was diagnosed with Stage 4 squamous cell carcinoma of the nasal cavity, basically nasal cancer. Our initial feelings and mood were, "He's too young for cancer! We work out at least four times a week! We try to eat healthy most of the week!" The doctors told us that sometimes the human body is funny in this way...well we weren't laughing. I was surprised that I didn't crumble or cry from the news, as a matter of fact, I had an outer body experience. I'm not sure if you believe in those types of things, but they have happened to me a couple times in my life. Another time I vividly remember having one is when my Pastor and the Officer came to notify us about the passing of my Dad. But as my body is sitting in the hard, cold, and metal chair, my mind and spirit seems to be floating in the air and looking down on me. I think it was calling out to my Dad and God at that moment, screaming "HELP! HELP ME! I DON'T KNOW WHAT TO DO!"

Being the protector and caregiver to my Mom and brother, while also acting in survival mode since my Dad passed, led me to put myself on the back burner and I had become complacent in life and work. You know that feeling when you become complacent, you become bored and lazy.

I've always had a go-getter attitude, but my spirit was broken. I had the awareness to realize my complacency, but never wanted to fully acknowledge it therefore, never having to act on it. It is interesting during this time, that even though I didn't even know what a caregiver was, I had become one! Up until this point, what I knew a caregiver to be was someone who helps their elderly parent. I didn't realize caregivers can be from different walks of life, different ages, and taking care of more than someone who is elderly or physically sick. I didn't even KNOW I was a caregiver back in 2011, until someone pointed it out to me. A caregiver often-times gets thrown into caregiving situations in a blink of an eye, with little to no regard of what she or he may already have on their plate.

I looked down on Troy and saw him total disbelief and shock. When I heard him cry out, "I don't want to die", I instantly snapped back into reality and turned to him to tell that we WILL FIGHT! I told Troy that I would help him fight cancer, no matter the cost. The doctor had excused himself so that he could figure out the next steps with other doctors, so when Troy and I had the room to ourselves that is when he started to cry. Troy was so scared that I was going to leave him in the dust after hearing this news, and once again I had to tell him that I would stand by him and fight. His doctor notified that we would need to see an oncologist at this point so speak about Troy's options on how to treat the cancer. Troy was upset, because like in the past, he thought he would have a surgery and it would be out and over. But unlike the past, this was cancer and it had cracked some of his skull bone and eaten away at some of his nasal bone, so they couldn't just go in and remove it easily. At that specific news, I was speechless and instantly saddened. I can't believe that much damage was happening to my fiancé right in front of my eyes and I didn't know it! Once we made the first appointment with Troy's oncologist, we were able to leave the Barrett

Cancer Center and breathing fresh air was so needed at that moment! When we initially heard the news, it was like all the air got sucked out of the room and what was left was hot and stale air. I almost felt like I was suffocating. I never would wish this experience on anyone, not even my worst enemy.

My brain was in such a fog by this point, I didn't know what to think! I was sad because our lives were going to change. Not sure what that change looked like, but I just knew what I had planned in my head for us, was not to be. I was angry because Troy was only 37 and we worked out regularly but so did my Dad, and then that started that whole hamster wheel of emotions. I wanted to scream because how dare cancer? Wasn't losing my Dad enough? Just the thought of losing my soon to be husband, made me ill. I also felt guilty. Why guilty, you say? Well because for a couple months, Troy had been complaining about headaches and had been having more frequent and severe nosebleeds but because I told him to self-medicate with cold compresses and Advil or Tylenol if it made him better then don't worry about going to the doctor. He put his trust in me and my words and look where it got him, look where it got US! I felt so foolish and that I had failed him, what a great fiancé I was turning out to be. I can't even make sure he stays healthy.

Our drive home was quiet. Normally on long drives we will listen to music nonstop and talk about our plans, etc. but that day, nothing. I remember earlier that day, we had discussed what we would have for dinner but now, dinner seemed like something that we might end up skipping that night. Two people who love food, couldn't even fathom eating at that point. I just knew I couldn't do this alone, but I didn't know anyone else who could help me that understood other than my Mom. We needed a plan and fast, or else these next few weeks and even months were going to be chaotic! My Mom, the wonderful woman that she is, called upon all the prayer warriors she knew. I've never seen her text and call people so fast in my life! It was amazing to watch her in that moment, because I remember having to do the same thing for her when my Dad died. When she couldn't speak or think, I spoke and thought for her and now in my weak moment she was repaying the love. I can't say enough, how wonderful my Mom is, and she deserves all the roses and accolades. Troy was added to multiple prayer request chains within hours, all due to my Mom's tenacity and fervor. The three of us prayed together and it is the first time that I remember seeing Troy openly pray.

I remember my Mom saying later the next day that she wanted Troy to move in with us. At that time Troy and I had lived separately at our parents' homes, until after the wedding so that we could save money for the wedding and honeymoon and all the wonderful things that occur during "regular" married life. I just knew Troy and I would have a new normal from now on and I would have to accept it, not that I didn't fight that acceptance. This hurt too, the unknowing of what was to come and what our new lives would look like. I believe my Mom sensed that and she has told me she felt so bad for me and that life is truly not fair, but I have her support in whatever I needed for me and Troy. The amount of love that she poured into me at that moment helped me move on and allowed me the space to focus on what Troy needed.

# CHAPTER 26:

## *"It Will All Be Worth It"*

-Mary Mary

W e met with the radiation oncologist the following week and we got to take a tour of the facility where Troy would be having treatment. This facility was a big deal because at the time, there were only about a dozen like it in the country. Due to the placement of the tumor, he was going to have to have a specialized radiation called proton therapy. Proton therapy is a type of radiation, but it delivers the radiation to a specific area using high beams to treat a specific location. Regular radiation therapy permeates throughout the whole area with harmful radiation rays to normal and healthy tissue. I believe proton radiation delivers 50-60% less harmful rays to healthy tissue, which was perfect for Troy's situation since the tumor was getting closer to his eye socket.

The facility was very impressive to see as well. The proton therapy machine was HUGE, they couldn't even show us the whole thing because it wrapped around the whole building. The nurses told us that it was made in Germany and when they shipped it to this facility, they had to shut down Interstate I-75 because of how big the parts are! Also, there are German engineers that are constantly monitoring the machine inside the building and virtually. They even have a nice waiting room for the caregivers and the receptionists were so accommodating and nice. Always offering something to drink and a snack, which I thought was courteous as most of the time caregivers are overlooked. Everyone seemed to be all smiles, which struck me as odd because we are in a hospital looking at this massive radiation machine, but their good nature was infectious, and we were happy that Troy would receive treatment here. Going through all our questions and as new ones came up along the tour, the nurses and doctor were able to help guide us on what a typical treatment session would look like. Once they described all these details, Troy and I felt comfortable that he was going to be receiving care from this hospital.

Unbeknownst to us, what we didn't realize is that we needed to also meet with an oncologist that specializes in chemotherapy. We were like WHY? He was due to start radiation within the next week due to the severity of his case, now we have one more setback! The radiation doctor explained to us that after the Cancer Board at U.C. Hospital met, they felt like it was the right move to have chemotherapy first due to the size of the tumor and the location. They had hoped that chemotherapy would shrink the tumor and therefore the proton therapy would be more successful. We really couldn't argue that, so we met with the chemo doctor. As we were nervously sitting in the examination room, waiting for the doctor to enter, Troy and I held hands and kept whispering to each other how much we loved one another. This was a scary time for us, we had this news that he had this devastating disease, but we still had to wait to hear how it would be treated and all kinds of exams and X-rays to be taken. We just wanted him to start some form of treatment so that he would begin to get better! HURRY UP

ALREADY! Well as I was turning that notion in my head, I hear the click clack of heels on the floor and the doorknob starts to turn. A short woman with short, brown hair, and a nice, warm smile entered the room.

She introduced herself and told us that she was not necessarily happy to see us in this predicament but that she would do whatever she can to shrink and/or eradicate Troy's tumor. We could tell right away that she wasn't going to play any games and she knew what she was doing. She had this aura about her that we knew we would be in good hands and that she would truly fight for Troy. She was very exact and firm in telling us what our options were and that they would be limited due to the size and where the tumor was located. The chemo doctor suggested the chemo drug Cisplatin, but she cautioned us that it would be the harshest drug, but it would be the most effective to treat his tumor. Troy told her whatever it would take for him to get rid of the tumor and have a fighting chance, because he wasn't ready to die. Troy kept such a great attitude and tenacity during the beginning of his treatment.

We didn't have to wait long for Troy's treatments to start, since they wanted to attack the tumor aggressively. Troy had to have a mini surgery to input a port in his chest, since he would receive chemo every day for five days a week for an undetermined amount of time. Inserting the port would save Troy from being stuck with a needle each day, as Troy HATES needles. The port acts as a gateway of some sorts for the chemo to flow through the body and it won't cause any harm or damage to the veins. A pharmacist came to talk to Troy and I about the different medications that he would be on and even gave me a calendar and clearly marked it there when I should give him his medicine. It was imperative that he take certain medications at specific times, so that he wouldn't have an adverse reaction to the chemo. There were so many pills, I instantly felt anxious just looking at the bottles, at one point he was on about six or seven different medications. I was so nervous that I was going to mess up and have a hand in him getting sick, Troy would always encourage me and tell me that he trusted me and that I am doing a good job. Troy and this pharmacist instantly connected over their love for Chicago and all the sports teams in Chicago. It made him comfortable, which made me happy. Even though his doctor informed us of the possible side effects, we didn't know what exactly to expect until Troy was in the "chemo or treatment chair" as he liked to call it.

The chemo chair was like a reclining massage chair you'd find at a nail salon, but without the massage function and of course, the pedicure. Troy loathed this chair, not necessarily because of the lack of comfort but because of the whole situation of why he must even be sitting there in that chair. I had to constantly remind him that that chair could possibly save his life and we must go and sit in it! I mean at least his chair was comfortable! Mine would start to hurt after a couple hours. Sometimes we would have to wait in the lobby of the cancer center because there were no chairs available and open for him to receive treatment. Now this could happen for a multitude of reasons, but Troy would get so upset if he couldn't get back there at his specific appointment time! In his mind, the earlier he got started, the earlier he could leave that horrid chair behind...until the next day.

After a couple of weeks, I started noticing that The Barrett Cancer Center was usually packed with people getting some sort of treatment. It was an interesting sight to see, I know of people who had cancer in the past, but I never had to be in the trenches with them, like I was now. It made my heart hurt for other families that had to go through this rotten disease or anything else, but I couldn't get over the fact that there were so MANY people! When we would enter, we would have to check in with the receptionist to get parking validation and then check in with billing. After all of that, depending upon if he had to have blood work done or not, Troy would have to wait in the blood clinic line, THEN we could go downstairs to the area in which they give out chemo treatment. We would always take the elevator from floor 2 to floor 1 and we started jokingly calling it "the dungeon" because we had to laugh to keep from crying, right? Downstairs wasn't really a dungeon at all, it was brightly lit, nurses and doctors smiling at you, and it really made you feel more comfortable for what you were about to walk into. We would have to check in with another receptionist desk to let them know that Troy was ready and then we would have to wait. Like I mentioned before, sometimes the wait could be two minutes or one time we waited about two hours to be asked to come into the chemo treatment room (Troy almost walked out of this particular appointment).

Now once we would get seated, Troy would get as comfortable as he could as a nurse would come around and introduce themselves and let us know that they would be taking care of him that day. They would begin to draw more blood and I remember Troy and I saying, is this the blood bank for vampires? I know they had to constantly take blood from him to check his vitals, so I'm glad he had a port because he wouldn't have done so well with all the needle pokes. Next, they would hook him up to saline solution so that he would stay hydrated because the Cisplatin could and would deplete him. They would also give Troy anti-nausea medicine so that he wouldn't get sick, because of how strong this medicine was. He would have chemo every day for five days a week, every three weeks with no end date given. All of this frightened me, but I knew we had no choice!

I remember some of my anxiety revolved around a little device that housed a drug called Neulasta. It was used after each time Troy finished chemo for that week, because chemo depletes your body of so many nutrients, your body can be left without white blood cells to fend off infections. The

Neulasta pod would inject his body with white blood cells. The reason why it worried me so was the fact that I would be left up to my own devices and skills to monitor it and make sure that the pod was working well and that I would have to take it off and dispose of it properly as well. The Neulasta pod couldn't be injected in his body until 24 hours AFTER his last chemo treatment, so that meant I was the nurse that would be on-call for the weekend. So, I was nervous about taking the pod off due to the lack of experience with medical devices, I wasn't sure about my skills. I didn't want to hurt Troy, and I didn't want to cause him any pain. I knew it was something that I had to do because his chemo was Monday through Friday, and because of having to wait 24 hours after his last chemo treatment, it was left to me to take it off. I would dramatically wash my hands up to my elbows and put some gloves on because I was so scared of possibly infecting him, which I didn't want those problems on top of the issues he already had. So, obviously I was extremely cautious. It was interesting because the Neulasta pod would beep, and it would beep so loud. It was almost scary, it would always make us jump, each time. That loud beep was the indicator that the white blood cells were being pumped back into his body. That Neulasta pod was necessary to offset any possible infection that might come, because the cisplatin depleted his white blood cell counts, so they needed to put him back into his body. When that pod would beep, we knew that the medicine would take about 45 minutes to permeate throughout his body. Then I would have to check the pod to make sure that all the medicine had been injected into Troy. And then that's when I would have to start taking the pod off, which, of course, I was nervous about.

But Troy, God love him, he would always reassure me that I was doing a good job, and he would let me know if I was hurting him. With any anxious feelings, most of the time it's all in your head, and despite all the anxious feelings, I did a great job of removing the Neulasta pod. It's important that the medical staff at his cancer treatment center did show me how to remove it, thankfully! I'm not going to lie; I was still nervous. It's one thing practicing with the professional, and then it's a whole different situation, when 24 to 48 hours later, YOU are responsible without the medical professional being there to help. In my mind I was saying repeatedly, "Am I doing this right? Oh no, what's going to happen if I mess this up?". It was a struggle at first, but because of how many treatments Troy had to go through I started getting the hang of it after the first couple times that I had to do it. Of course, this was just the beginning of his treatment and all the things that I was going to learn along the way.

At first, I didn't realize how much it was going to cost us to go back and forth like we were doing. The gas and wear and tear on our car were starting to add up and to make matters worse, the car that we had in the beginning of his treatment phase was a leased car. Yeah, I could only drive so many miles each month, well as you could guess, we blew through those miles! When I got that car lease, I wasn't expecting for our life to turn out like it was, but here we were! The amazing thing about God is, he hears your cry even if you don't think He does! Little did we know a few women at my Mom's job were planning a wonderful coin auction benefit for Troy. It's amazing how people who have never met Troy wanted to help him through this process, financially. I'm still overwhelmed by the outpouring of love. The amount of donations that were to be auctioned off at the benefit amazed me. So many people and local businesses donated because of the relationship they had with my parents or myself.

Even Troy's old boss donated an item to be auctioned off. I finally got to meet some of Troy's family members during that auction and I kept telling them that I was sorry it took for this moment for us to meet, but at least we met! That room was filled with so much love and hope, it almost made the windows bust open! I remember making a declaration that night in front of those people, that Troy and I would fight until they declared him cancer free because cancer can't have him! My heart believed this to be true, but of course my nervous mind wandered. That auction raised about $4,000 and we just cried when they tallied everything up! We couldn't believe it. We praised God and sent thank you cards to everyone who had donated and even put a thank you letter in the newspaper for all the local businesses to see! We were so hopeful that things would start to improve for Troy.

Once the doctors saw Troy's chemo was effective, meaning that the knot on his forehead was reducing in size, they felt comfortable with him starting the proton radiation therapy. The proton therapy seemed to go on forever because, unlike chemotherapy which was Monday through Friday every three weeks five days a week, proton therapy was every day, each week. We were having to drive each way every day, either to Northern Cincinnati, or near downtown Cincinnati. Either way, we were beating the highway every single day five days a week for an uncertain amount of time. We weren't told when this treatment was going to be over because it was up to Troy's body and the tumor. His doctors were striving for the goal of a cure. They couldn't promise us anything, but they told us this numerous times that they were looking to cure Troy and that is the hope that we lived on each week and month. They couldn't really give us a timeframe; it was just how his body reacted to the chemo-therapy and the radiation. We lived anywhere from an hour to an hour and 30 minutes away from the U.C. Hospital chain that he had his treatments at. Oftentimes, his treatment days were full days due to traffic, breaks in between treatment, etc. oh and don't get me started on the traffic!

Little known fact about me, even though I love hopping in my car and taking off to new places, I actually HATE driving! Yeah so of course, this part of my life felt like a lesson on patience (which used to be nonexistent) because if the traffic was bad or there were accidents, we may end up late or rushing. A lot of time in the car was spent praying, listening to music, dancing, and going over what we felt in that moment. Our car rides were very entertaining, which we had to make them that way or else we would have lost our minds. I'm sure to people on the outside looking inside of our car, we probably did look like we had lost our minds, but we had to entertain ourselves to keep from crying. We really tried our best to be positive throughout this process, but sometimes that's all we had was the laughter in the most random and odd times. Anything to keep from crying.

Before Troy's first treatment he had to be fitted for his proton therapy mask. It was the mask that he had to wear that matched up with their computer system which would be able to pinpoint the specific areas where the proton therapy beams were going to hit his face. The whole technical and scientific side to the proton therapy was very fascinating, as well as overwhelming. When Troy showed me his mask that he had to wear it looked like something that Hannibal Lecter would have worn in the movie, *Silence of the Lambs* and he even had to go inside of a tube and recline down like Hannibal did in an iconic scene in the movie. It covered his full head down to his shoulders and it was like a hard plastic material that had to be strapped tightly to his face. There could be no wiggle room due to the preciseness needed for this treatment. The radiation would start early in the morning, we preferred early mornings so that we could have the rest of our day to either go to the other location for his chemotherapy or return home. Troy liked the days when we only had to go to radiation so that we could go back home, and he could rest. Having both chemo and radiation on the same day zapped him of his energy. It was hard to see him like this because we used to be avid runners. We would easily run anywhere from two to four miles almost every day, and to see him go from that type of energy to little to no energy was so disheartening. It made me sad and thwarted my motivation and desire to run because it had become "our" thing. Even though running started as my thing that helped me through my grief with my Dad's passing, it turned into something that Troy and I enjoyed together, and I was sad at the thought of permanently losing that. The things that cancer treatment, and cancer period, makes you go through. All the physical, mental, and spiritual changes that cancer makes you go through, it can be very devastating. we didn't have a choice. I know I keep saying that throughout this book but literally we, we didn't have a choice. We didn't have time to get a second or third opinion, when the doctor said, jump! we asked how high? We had to do what we had to do.

With each treatment and/or drug that they introduced to Troy's plan, the doctors would tell us the benefits and the consequences for each one. Proton therapy's benefits outweighed the consequences for us, but we still knew about the consequences. Due to the placement of the tumor, the consequences of the proton therapy were reddening and tightening of the skin near the radiation exposure area. He could have lost his eyesight, had headaches, and possible ringing in the ears. When you are in the fight for your life, you don't really think about all the consequences until afterwards or because you can visibly see it happening. Due to receiving proton therapy in his head and neck region, Troy lost saliva. The loss of saliva has detrimental effects to your dental hygiene, which is something that we didn't account for, but some cancer patients must deal with it. Troy lost the full mobility of his mouth, meaning he can only open it his mouth about 25-30% like he used to. He cannot normally eat a hamburger and watching him eat reminds me that I should never take my good health for granted. I can easily open my mouth to eat a juicy 5 Guys burger, but Troy cannot. He must cut things up into smaller pieces so that he can fit the things into his mouth. Troy does mouth exercises that will help him open his mouth, and keep it open, as far as he can, and he must constantly rinse out his mouth because of the dry mouth. Radiation totally zapped his mouth dry, which made me realize how important saliva is to your mouth! Saliva protects your teeth, because it gets the bacteria out of your mouth, and helps with digestion. Of course, we noticed these changes over a course of time, and I would have to remind Troy when he should be taking rinsing out his mouth and doing his mouth exercises. I felt more like his Mom than his significant other. The side effects from the radiation were one thing, but we never saw what was coming after taking a break from chemo and radiation.

I will say, a cool thing about the radiation treatment center are the doctors, nurses, and receptionists were amazing. They made Troy feel good, he got to choose his own music or podcast that he would like to listen to while he was getting his treatment. Even though it's not something we wanted to do or someplace that we wanted to be, he felt welcomed and well cared for. As his caregiver, that is all that I could hope for. I cared more about his well-being than I did my own. I was his ride or die, in it to win it!

During this time of treatment, I was told to go speak with an American Cancer Society (ACS) representative through the hospital for any help that I may need. I wasn't even SURE of what I needed, which I know many caregivers can relate to, but I decided what could I possibly lose? Come to find out there are organizations and charities that provide gas or grocery gift cards to those who are battling cancer, and even more specifically, head/neck cancer like Troy. I always wanted to thank those individuals but most of them wanted to stay anonymous. There was even an organization that was willing to pay rent/mortgage and utilities for one month for those in treatment, that was such a blessing! The ACS representative even mentioned that during the weeks he was receiving both treatments, that we could possibly stay at the Hope Lodge. She gave me a brochure to look at what they offer and to think about it. Once Troy and I met with the manager at the Hope Lodge and had a tour, we decided to give it a try. It was free to us, we just had to pick up after ourselves and behave in a respectable manner which was no problem.

The American Cancer Society offered the Hope Lodge to anyone who was in treatment and their loved ones, who lived more than 70 miles away from U.C. Hospital. The Hope Lodge was so beneficial for us because it was about 5-10 minutes away from the main hospital that Troy was seen at. When you first pull up to the Hope Lodge you can admire the grand stature of the place, it almost reminded me of a castle like fortress. The only thing that was missing was a moat and knight with his shining armor. It was huge, it sits on a corner on a busy street, so it was interesting to see the differences in the surroundings versus the building. Troy wasn't pleased, he thought it was creepy on the outside and kept saying this looked like a place that we had seen in movies where a serial killer would reside. When you step inside this massive property, it reminds you of how old it is. It reminded me of Disney's Haunted Mansion ride and movie. When you would walk around the lobby and even going up and down the stairs the floor would creak and moan. Troy was not wanting to have to stay there, and there were times where he would ask me if we could just go home to our bed. I would have to explain to him that this is for a week or two due to his treatment schedule and me also working full time. Working from my computer full time was a blessing but being in that old building had its challenges with the lack of a strong Wi-Fi signal, oftentimes I would have to take Troy to the hospital an hour or two early just so I could get a better signal there. And you guessed it, he was also not happy about that! I know it was from the lack of restful sleep, because he didn't sleep very well there but I would also explain to him that it was for our own good.

The nights where he couldn't sleep, he would wake me up and ask me to drive him around. I would ask him why he couldn't sleep, and it would range from being in the Hope Lodge to the steroids they put him on, to the sleep medication they prescribed for him. Let me tell you another story about having to advocate for your loved one's health. The doctors prescribed Ambien to help Troy fall asleep since we had mentioned that he wasn't sleeping well. The first weekend that I had to help him with his chemo pump plus the Neulasta pod, we were in bed at the Hope Lodge, and I was getting that GOOD GOOD sleep! Like the sleep that you haven't had in YEARS, and all the sudden Troy wakes me up in a panic. Naturally, I start panicking too, he's shouting "BABE THERE'S A BOMB! THERE'S A BOMB ATTACHED TO ME, HELP ME GET IT OFF NOWWWWWW!" I looked at him and then I noticed that he was holding his chemo pump bag in his hands and I told him to settle down and that there was no bomb. Troy gets even more panicked and yells again, "ASHLEY HELP ME DIFFUSE THE BOMB!". I get up out of bed and I look him in the eye, and I tell him, "Lay your butt back in the bed or else you will have more issues to worry about than MF a bomb!". (Momma J and Momma Sharon, don't judge me but I said a few expletive words in that moment). I must have said it with so much force because I put the fear in him, and he laid back down. The next morning, we were scheduled to see his chemo doctor for a follow up that following Tuesday and I was so happy to see her, because she could even start to examine Troy, I told her what had happened and to please take him off that pill. She asked if I was sure, and I told her YES and Troy even acknowledged that he didn't want to be on it.

I remember that I would have to drive him around at night to fall asleep, like a baby. I knew he would have rather been in the comfort of his own bed at home, but I had to explain to him that I was just too tired and that I couldn't risk driving us home. So, we would stay at the Hope Lodge, especially on the weeks where he would have chemo AND radiation. When he had his first major surgery, I was able to stay there as well during his recovery phase. The rooms that were at the Hope Lodge were kind of creepy, enormous, but comfortable. Each room had their own bathroom, which was nice and the only thing that was shared were like the common areas where there was a TV, and the kitchen/dining room. They provided areas in the fridge and pantry for everyone to have their own shelves and space. I cooked many of our meals, because I was trying to watch what Troy was eating and making sure he was getting the best nutrition possible. I remember they had a theater room, and Troy and I had our own movie night, which gave us a sense of normalcy, even though it wasn't normal. It was very comforting, and I know he didn't like being there, because he equated the Hope Lodge with cancer. He would remember all the times he got sick and didn't feel well and it became one with the Hope Lodge.

I remember one evening he got sick, and I mean it was coming out of both ends! Troy was vomiting and pooping at the same time, so I had to help him clean himself up so I had taken off my engagement ring and set it up on the refrigerator so that I wouldn't mess it up. there. I guess I must have forgotten about it, until a couple days went by and Troy brought it to my attention. He asked where my engagement ring was and I said, "oh it's, it's in the room or whatever, I think?". I started thinking in my head, "Where did it go? Where did I last see it?", because I had no clue. I went down to the kitchen at the Hope Lodge and searched through the kitchen. I searched through our room and throughout the common areas and couldn't find it! I told the manager at the Hope Lodge and the cleaning ladies about my lost engagement ring, and I showed them pictures. I was so distraught; I couldn't believe that I lost one of the most important things that Troy had ever given me. He was so sweet (or maybe it was the chemo talking) and he said, "Hey we'll worry about getting a new one after I get through this treatment. Can we just focus on that for now?". Of course, I gladly obliged! The engagement ring was something that could be replaced. I kept apologizing because it took a lot for him to buy that ring for me and it was incredibly special. It was perfect, everything that I had ever dreamed of plus more. I mean it was princess cut, Disney Princess Bride things. The ring was missing for about two weeks and it came time for us to leave the Hope Lodge to go back home and stay home. As I emptied out the trash cans to clean up our room, I noticed a flash of rose gold and dug some more and at that the bottom of the trash can, was my ring. Somehow, I must have bumped the refrigerator and the ring slid into the trash can. We were so relieved, I cried because by that time the ring had been missing for two weeks. Then I called my Mom to let her know the good news! She screamed in delight and she said, "Hold onto it. I'm coming down right now to get it!" and sure enough, my Mom drove an hour and a half to come get my ring! She took it back to her house and she was going to get it insured that night. My Mom said, I wasn't going to get it back in until I became more responsible, and of course Troy agreed.

Our last day at the Hope Lodge for that week was the next day, which Troy was incredibly happy about. Like I mentioned before he really didn't like staying there so the stretches of a week or two that we had to be there, I don't think he slept very well, but the Hope Lodge was a necessity for us. We ended up staying there the weeks that he would have chemo and radiation because of the proximity to the hospital. Having the opportunity to make home cooked meals away from home, instead of grabbing fast food was so imperative. The Hope Lodge was a necessary and vital, important part of Troy's treatment, and the American Cancer Society deserves all the accolades for having it for cancer patients and their families. I forever will be grateful for it and the time we had to spend there.

May 7, 20217, Troy graduated with his Associates degree in Business Management from Sinclair Community College. He had just finished a round of chemo and was feeling sick and weak, but he was adamant about attending the actual ceremony. I got in contact with the student services office to implore for Troy to either get called up first or seated close to the stage. He was able to sit close to the stage and take bathroom breaks as desired. My Mom, Grandpa and I were all in attendance for Troy's big moment and we all couldn't have been prouder! Not only had he accomplished his goal of getting a degree, but he also did it while in treatment! He is my hero!

When we got to June 2017, the doctors wanted to give his body a break from all the chemo and radiation. We took the opportunity to take Troy's daughter to Disney World, as she had never been, and we wanted to show her where her Dad asked me to marry him. Troy and I were so excited to get out of Ohio and take her to our happy place. She was so excited to fly on a plane and see Mickey Mouse. We only had enough time to go to Disney for one day, so we chose to go to Magic Kingdom, so she (we) could see as many Disney Princesses as possible! It was overwhelming but so joyous to see her reaction to everything at Magic Kingdom. We happened to go on one of the hottest days it seemed like, I believe we ended up spending about $100 in drinks alone so we could stay hydrated. Of course, going with an eight-year-old, we bought all the shiny objects she wanted and all the cotton candy, and Mickey Mouse shaped ice cream. We really enjoyed our time, despite having to stand in line in the hot sun. I noticed that Troy was getting really red and sweaty, and he looked like he was about to pass out. We immediately headed to the

Haunted Mansion ride since it is one of my favorites, but more importantly, it is inside and air conditioned. I was so excited to share these moments with Troy and my soon to be stepdaughter.

In August 2017, Troy and I went to Fort Lauderdale to celebrate his graduation and have time for ourselves. We wanted to have fun and do all the fiancé and engagement stuff that we missed out on in the beginning of the year! His doctors thought he was making great progress and we were making some headway on wedding planning; everything was great! I've never seen him wear so much sunblock in my life, but due to him getting overheated and burnt at Disney, he didn't want to take any chances. We ate and drank, spent almost each day at the beach, and even rented a car for a day and drove to South Beach. That area was too jam packed for Troy's taste and I could tell that he was ready to get back to Fort Lauderdale after we finished lunch. I remember constantly looking in his baby blue eyes and just falling more and more in love with him. I often reflect on those moments and smile, but I also hurt because of everything we've gone through so far, and I didn't realize the devastation that was to come our way soon.

# CHAPTER 27:

## *"Fear"*

-Lecrae

**D**ear Cancer,
Why did you enter my life? You turned it upside down and inside out.

Why did you pick my loved one? Making him hurt so much and I wish I could take the pain away from him.

Why did you change the course of our lives? We just got engaged and at the top of the world.

Why did you make me feel so lonely? I felt lonely even in a crowded room with doctors, nurses, and my loved one.

Why did you have to make me see my loved one at his lowest and weakest? I hadn't even taken the vow "even in sickness and health" but here I am.

Why did you take his dignity? The poop, vomit, and other bodily fluids I had to continually clean was not fun.

Why do you constantly cause me anxiety and stress? You will always be lurking in the shadows and his cancer status can easily change at ANY moment.

Why did you make me realize who my real friends are?

Cancer makes your REAL friends step up and step out for you!

Why is so much pressure put on me but there's no support for ME? I was often lost during his treatment and even though there's social workers for you, YOU (the caregiver) are left to your own devices to seek them out.

Why can't I take care of myself? I often feel guilty for taking care of my own needs, thus thrusting me into burnout.

Why did I worry about what others would think so much? I was so worried that I was failing as a caregiver and that his family thought I was weak.

Why are you laughing at me? During his treatment, there were times that the tumor would shrink then it would grow again and almost double in size. I almost felt like you were laughing at me from inside his body.

Why did you make me hate his body so? I had to shift my mindset to understanding that I was mad at his body for failing him and NOT HIM.

Why do you make Troy question his very existence? I know Troy wonders why cancer affected him and not his brothers. I know that hurts him and has made him question what he should be doing with his life, I know he is on the right path to discovering it and I have no doubt that he will have the last laugh.

Why have you affected so many of my loved ones? I have lost one too many loved ones in my life to this disease. I won't let you take one more.

Why did you make me question myself? Oftentimes I would question my decisions that I would have to help him make on behalf of his own care. Constant murmurs of my anxiety and running thoughts, manifested itself into stomach ulcers and migraines.

Why did you make me question God? I wondered, how

could God not only take my Daddy away but allow the man I want to spend my forever with, also die? How could that be? It was so frustrating and enraging.

Why do you leave me with so many unanswered questions? Literally makes my head spin and my heart hurt.

# CHAPTER 28:

## "*When You Believe*"

-Whitney Houston & Mariah Carey

November 1-7, 2017, I went to Colombia on a solo trip before Troy's next doctor's visit. I needed time to rejuvenate and be carefree by myself! I really enjoyed my time in Colombia. It was amazing, everything from the food, culture, people, beaches, and the drinks, they had everything I needed! What made this trip so special is because I got to visit two Colombian girls I met on my trip to Egypt. They showed me around their city of Bogota, which is the capital, which was made famous or infamous after the Netflix series, Narcos. It was neat to walk around the city and breathe everything in, Ohio had become so stifling for me. I dreaded going back, especially when my Mom told me that she thought the knot on Troy's forehead was growing again.

When I returned to the U.S. and I saw Troy, I knew that there was a legitimate concern. I called Troy's chemo doctor and asked if he could be seen because it had been about three to four months without treatment. He couldn't be seen until the next week due to the Thanksgiving holiday, which was an excruciating wait. She looked at him with some concern as well, and she ordered for Troy to have another MRI. We had to wait on the MRI results which would take a couple days, but I had already arranged for my Mom and I to look at wedding gowns, and Troy and I to take our engagement pictures that weekend that we had to wait. Having those events planned for that exact weekend was a blessing in disguise because we would've sat at home, worried sick if we didn't have that planned. Despite all the wedding festivities planned for that weekend, I just knew that we probably wouldn't be receiving good news. I kept an upbeat and positive mindset, but it was extremely hard. I cried during my dress fitting and not because I found MY dress, but for the fact that my Dad wasn't going to be able to walk me down the aisle nor was I sure that I would have someone to walk down the aisle to. It was a beautiful moment that was stained by anxiety of Troy's test results.

My Mom and I went down to Cincinnati's Reading Bridal District to try on dresses, and I had no desire to buy a dress that day due to wanting to take my time, and I refused to be that girl that bought her first dress at the first location that she went shopping in. I had not tried on any dresses at all yet, but I did know I wanted a Princess ball gown type. I wanted to get as close to a Disney Princess bride experience as possible! I had made a reservation at two different places, but I was a little upset since it would only be my Mom and I in attendance. I wanted that full experience that you see on the wedding shows, but most of my bridesmaids lived out of the state so they couldn't come. As we entered the store, I saw a bride-to-be trying on dresses with her entourage of six ladies, and she looked overwhelmed and unhappy. I heard them all saying different things to the bride-to-be about the dress she had on and I felt bad for her. When my Mom and I meet my sales lady, she helps me peruse the ball gown selection and pull some dresses to try on. The first dress was made of a newer crinkle type fabric with dazzling beading at the top. It reminded me of a hipper type of Cinderella ball gown, the dress fit my curves in all the right areas. Hugged me tight where it needed to and flowed out in the areas that I wanted to hide. I intuitively knew that Troy would lose his mind when he saw me in it, and I secretly loved it too.

I remember Facetiming my cousin so she could see a part of the dress and she started crying. I had to remind myself to keep my composure because I wasn't 100% sure if this was the one or not. Again, I didn't want to say yes to the first dress I tried on! I tried on three more dresses and my smile began to diminish with each dress I tried on, until finally I told my Mom that I was through. I didn't want to do this anymore. She called for the sales lady to help me out of the last dress and when she unhooked that last button, I started sobbing. I told the lady that I was sorry, but I had a lot on my mind. I was dealing with the loss of my Dad and the fact that he wouldn't be there to walk me down the aisle, and that the man I wanted to marry is in limbo with cancer, also not to add, that I wanted more of my bridesmaids with me. All these emotions that I had kept bottled in were spilling out, in the middle of the dressing room with this lady that I had just met and my Mom standing outside the dressing room door. Not how I expected this dress shopping trip to go.

The sales lady told me that I should get dressed again and go sit down in the main area of the bridal shop, she would go get a couple glasses of wine and meet my Mom and I. The lady took her time to explain that having "only" my Mom with me is actually one of the smartest things that brides-to-be could do so that they can listen to their own intuition, and not have to fight through too many voices and sugges-tions. She allowed me to tell my story of the sudden loss of my Dad, and the possibility that I may be getting a dress for a wedding that may or may not be happening based upon my fiancé's cancer diagnosis. She sat and listened to me, even passed another bridal gown fitting to a different sales lady, so that she could give me her full attention and care. After talking and having two glasses of wine, she asked me if there was at least ONE dress I liked or even loved. I told her the very first dress I tried one, so she suggested that I put it back on and see if I like it. With a renewed sense of eagerness, I agreed. When I put that dress on for the SECOND time, I KNEW it was the one! I instantly started crying, which in turn made my Mom cry. I just knew that I felt sexy and magnificent in this dress and it had to be mine! I ended up cancelling the next bridal shop we were due to go to, because there was no need to go there! I happened to be "that girl" who picked her first dress that she ever tried on to be her fairytale wedding dress. I believe that the sales lady was my angel in disguise, she wasn't even supposed to be working that day but got called in. I'll never forget her and her tenderness and kindness because you never know what someone is going through and she really helped me find some light amid my darkness.

The next day, Troy and I were due to take our engagement pictures. It was a cold November day and of course I just HAD to wear this beautiful purple peplum, one shoulder dress. I was excited because I had picked out a couple romantic spots for our engagement photos, but I could also tell that Troy was hurting that day. His headaches had come back and the knot on his nose had grown back with a vengeance, which made him self-conscious. The woman who did my makeup, which is like an older sister, did my makeup and then applied some to his nose and cheek area so that it wouldn't look so red and prominent. Our photographer happened to be like a little sister to me too and she did so well with the situation we presented to her. Troy felt more comfortable doing shots where he could hide the left side of his face, so none of our engagement photos are straight on both of our faces. She would help position us so that Troy felt confident, and we had fun, despite the situation and bitter cold! I remember my Mom would throw a blanket over my shoulders when our photographer wasn't taking pictures. My utmost favorite picture was the one that she took of us outside an old movie theater that had a marquee sign. We were able to take one of those iconic pictures where Troy dipped me, while kissing me, and my foot kicked up in the air! That kiss literally took my breath away, and I knew that whatever the doctor was going to tell us that we would get through it together!

That following Tuesday when we met with his chemo doctor, she confirmed that the MRI showed that the tumor was in fact growing back. Obviously, the treatment that they had done wasn't effective enough, so she suggested that they perform surgery on Troy at this point. We were referred to a surgeon who specializes in head and neck cancer patients. I wasn't that excited about surgery. I was terrified, anything can go wrong in surgery, right? But what choice did we have? We didn't have any choice, Troy had done the Cisplatin 9 times, and at this point he had completed about 17 proton treatments.

We met with several doctors to have consults and discuss the consequences versus the benefits of surgery. Each time we went to a different doctor, I had my questions ready to ask. It was like playing 20 Questions, except this wasn't a game. I'm sure caregivers can relate to all the questions that we have to ask on behalf of our loved ones. So here again, I find myself questioning everything just so I was clear and could help Troy make an informed decision about his surgery. Here is a sample of the questions that I had typed up in my phone to ask:

*How long is the healing process?*

*How long will Troy be in the hospital?*

*If an eye must be removed, how does a prosthetic eye work? Will he be fitted for one right after surgery? Or later?*

*Where does skin come from to fill in his nose?*

*Will there be pain in the eye area if it's removed?*

*How should we prepare for the procedure?*

*How long will the surgery take?*

*What kind of anesthesia will be used during the surgery? Will he be asleep during the surgery?*

*What can he expect after the surgery?*

*What possible complications can develop after surgery?*

*Will he need any special prep before surgery? Diet, medicine, blood work?*

*Will he need any pain meds to go home with? What can he do to help his recovery?*

*Have you performed this type of surgery before?*

I asked anything from A to Z because I wanted to make sure that it was the best thing for Troy and that he would recover well. Troy really liked the ENT specialist that would also be doing his reconstruction. Troy also felt amazingly comfortable with the surgeon, so we got the surgery scheduled. His first invasive surgery was going to be the day after his birthday, December 28th, 2017. My Grandpa, Mom, and Troy's Mom all came with me to sit in the hospital through the surgery. They all said I looked tired, and it was true, because the night before I kept coaxing Troy to go to sleep and then I would just watch him. I kept praying for his strength for the surgery the next day. We both were scared, but we just held each other close and tight that night! We literally didn't know what was going to happen the next day!

We had to be at the hospital at 5am, for the check-in process for surgery prep. I remember holding Troy's hands and asking if he wanted to talk with my Mom or his Mom. At some point, the surgeon, ENT, and neurosurgeon entered the room, and we weren't expecting a neurosurgeon but due to the tumor's proximity to the skull, they realized that they would have to cut into the skull area. So Troy was going to have three doctors in the operating room with him in, and I felt noticeably confident and comfortable with these doctors. After my Mom and I prayed with him for a successful surgery, the doctors wheeled him back to the operating room. It felt like a scene from a movie, I held onto his hand and at the last second, I let go and told him I love you. It was in God's hands at that moment! Little did I know that was going to be the last time I saw him before his new normal.

As we were all sitting in the family waiting room, it seemed surreal like it wasn't really happening. This wasn't our real life. I knew that this was going to be a long surgery, they had predicted anywhere from six to eight hours. As I sat back in the waiting room and looked around, there were so many people in it, and again, I was amazed at how many people have ailments which brings them to this point. These experiences continually opened my mind to be more aware of my own body and how you treat yourself (or don't). I didn't really have time to focus on me solely, even though I went on my travels throughout 2017, I still couldn't solely focus on me. I was constantly checking in and stressing. Almost regretting that I even left but having to sit in the waiting room made me think and I became more aware of the reality that this could be me in my future if I don't take care of myself. But who are we kidding? My total focus was on Troy.

So, when we were sitting there, the seats were comfortable at first but as the hours tick by the chairs become more and more hard. And it's hard to get comfortable. We had lively conversation throughout the first couple of hours, but as the hours kept dragging on, you got more and more quiet. I took solace in those quiet hours and would text my family and friends who cared so much about Troy and his well-being. In the late afternoon, my Mom and Troy's Mom excused themselves to go get food for all of us and no sooner did they leave, then I saw Troy's favorite doctor approaching me. He sat right next to me and my Grandpa was to the left of me. He told me that Troy was doing well in surgery, but unfortunately the tumor had cracked through his nostril and skull bone and was starting to eat away at the eye canal area. He told me that they had to remove Troy's left eye, even though it was still fully functional, since they believe, this tumor would keep coming back if they didn't. He apologized as he knew that all of this was such a shock, but it was so necessary. Troy and I knew that this could happen, but it happened was a whole different story.

I found myself not showing too much emotion, but I did look over at my Grandpa, and he just grabbed my hand and held it tight. My Grandpa, the sweet soul he is, said, "Baby, at least Troy is ALIVE! Sometimes we don't understand what happens in life, but we have to trust God that He is mighty and loving." I remember nodding in agreement, because if I spoke it might have come out as a howling cry. I ended up calling my mom and I told her what had happened, I heard her tell my soon to be mother-in-law and I hear them both crying. When they got back from getting food, I was trying to muster up the strength that I was going to need before seeing Troy in recovery. I told Troy's mom that this was a possible outcome of his surgery, but she was so distraught. Troy and I were in survival mode, we had to do what we had to do. Along the way, if things happened that we couldn't control, we would figure it out, but he wanted to survive by any means necessary!

I had lost my appetite, but knew I needed to eat before going to see Troy. It was the weirdest feeling ever. When he got to the ICU unit, it wasn't just a normal ICU unit, it was for burn victims. Due to the trauma that Troy went through, he had to be under extra special care. As I was preparing myself to see my fiancé, I kept wondering what I was going to see, but nothing was ever going to prepare me for what I was about to see. We had to walk down this long corridor and two different sets of doors and get buzzed into the burn unit, it seemed like we were walking into a fortress. When

I walked into that room, with his Mom on my side and my Mom behind me, all I saw were these machines hooked up to him and beeping with tubes sticking out of his head, stitches where his eye used to be, because they had to take skin from his back to put on his left eye area. Troy's face was bloody and beat up from the trauma of surgery. It was almost like Dr. Frankenstein's lair, but instead this was the love of my life and not a monster.

That moment I fully saw what had happened to Troy, I almost fainted. Thankfully, my Mom was right behind me to catch me. My Mom was always catching me and helping me through my whole caregiving journey. She was there to support me and catch me when I was falling. I will always give my mom her roses, because despite her own loss, she helped me. I had to step out into the hallway, because that room felt like all the oxygen had been sucked out and I was going to suffocate. I even remember gasping for air. I stepped out in the hallway because I didn't want Troy to see me cry or in that state of despair, once again...caregivers aren't "supposed" to show weakness or fear, right? Once I gathered my composure and went back into his room, I grabbed him by the hand, and I told him I loved him. Troy was saying how much he wanted to go home, but I told him that he couldn't go home. I tried explaining to Troy that he had to stay in the hospital because he just had surgery, and he kept asking when the doctors were going to take the patch off his eye. I remember having to painstakingly remind him that the doctors had to take his eye, but that they got the tumor out! When it was time for visitors to leave the area, Troy's Mom asked him if he wanted her to stay and I looked at her perplexed. At that moment, I realized that when Troy lost his eye(sight), that's when hers were finally opened. It took for his loss for her to see the complexity, the hurt, and fear that Troy had been going through in the past year.

# CHAPTER 29:

## "*Superwoman*"

-Alicia Keys

A fter I told the three of them goodbye, I got situated because I was going to stay in the hospital room with him. The nurses brought me a recliner chair that was a makeshift bed, and blankets and a pillow. I didn't want to leave his side, especially if he woke up in the middle of the night and looked for me. Troy's cousin reached out to me to see if it was ok if he and some other family members came to visit Troy a couple days after his surgery and I said yes, because that would give me a chance to get out of the hospital for the day. My dear friend, who lives in Cincinnati kept telling me that I needed to take care of myself and she kept saying "treat yo self". She finally kept emphasizing it, so I told her that I would go out for the day.

At first, I was like doesn't she know that I can't treat myself? Half of Troy's face has been dramatically changed, but sure I will go and have some fun while he is laid up in the hospital bed. Once Troy's family arrived and I spoke with them outside of Troy's hospital room to tell them the gritty details of his situation and what the future may look like, I excused myself to go get picked up by my friend. When she pulled up, I opened the door and got in and instantly let out this huge sigh. I tried not to shed a tear, but it felt so good to get out of the stifling hospital air. The air where I was constantly reminded of what cancer had done, not only to Troy but to me too! Cancer took OUR lives away and now we were going to have to figure out what that meant for our future, but at that moment, I was going on a spa day with my friend.

My friend could automatically sense my mood and energy was off and she asked how I was feeling. I didn't know exactly how to answer because I didn't want to complain, but I wanted to tell my truth, so I just said, "tired". Which I was tired, but also angry, disappointed, and blamed myself for Troy and I being in the predicament. Little did I know that that surgery was starting a slow burn out stage in my life. Because I was so busy with my own introspection, I don't remember what my friend was asking me but when I remember pulling up to the spa and we both had great anticipation. This was SO necessary! I used to get massages all the time but couldn't find the time to because I was running Troy everywhere. My friend had set us up with a foot detox bath, then an infrared sauna treatment, and finally topped off with one of the best massages EVER! I had never done a foot detox bath, but it was interesting to see the water change colors and just imagine that it was getting rid of any toxins that I had. Same with the infrared sauna, I got to sweat off any toxins that I had, and I felt as if I was releasing bad vibes and energy and then that massage gave me life. After our amazing spa experience, she took me to this delicious Japanese restaurant called *Quan Hapa* and I wanted to try one of everything! We had the most delectable ramen, okonomiyaki (Japanese pancake filled with green onion, bacon, mayo, & egg), and I washed it down with some sake.

On the way back to the hospital, I felt a sense of dread.

I almost wanted to ask her to drive back to her house, so I wouldn't have to go back up to the nightmare that had become my life in the blink of an eye. My friend kept reminding me to treat myself from time to time, because it is a healthy thing to do. I said, "yeah sure, I'll work on that", without any real conviction. I already felt a twinge of guilt for being away from Troy for so long, and what would his brother and cousin think? Why couldn't I just do something for myself without those guilty feelings? What I do know, is the fact that my friend saved me that day. I was in the deep end of the pool of despair (which I didn't realize was actually caregiver burnout) and she was able to bring me out of it, even for half a day! I will always appreciate and love her for that day. I don't know how my friend knew what I needed, but I'm so glad that she did! For my friend that might have seemed small, but to me that spa day was so special because I needed to leave the hospital and be away from all the beeping machines and bloody tubes that were running from Troy's head.

Whatever perfect life I had envisioned for Troy and I was thrown out the window within mere minutes, after his cancer diagnosis. I was 31 years old and newly engaged; I mean come on! I was angry because I had lost my Dad when I was 25 years old, and now the second man that I deeply loved was faced with a terminal illness. Early on in Troy's fight I tried not to let my anger show, but as time went on and there did not seem to be a light at the end of the tunnel I would lash out. I was angry at Troy's body, at God, and myself. I started to resent the fact that I was once again placed in a situation of being the strong woman, who makes sure that everyone else is taken care of. BUT WHAT ABOUT ME? Who takes care of the caregiver?

I know when someone is diagnosed with a terminal or chronical illness, it is about them, but it is also about the caregiver(s) in their lives. Most people do not check in on the caregiver, especially when they seem so strong...like me. It may be tough, but every hero has their downfall. Again, not to say that I didn't have a great support system, because I did. Most caregivers tend to internalize their feelings, so that they do not come off as a Negative Nancy or depressed. This is where I wish I would've had a therapist during Troy's treatment stages, so I could've found some healthier ways to work through my frustrations and emotions.

At first, I thought I resented Troy, but it wasn't him that I resented. I resented his body! The way that his body was being attacked by cancer and how it couldn't fight it off without these powerful drugs and beams of radiation that I knew would have everlasting effects on Troy. What choice did I really have in the matter? Instead of dwelling on resentment, I came to the realization that I had to change my mindset. It is not like Troy asked for cancer, it chose him for whatever reason. These are the cards that we had been dealt and we either must choose to fight or flight! Of course, we chose to fight, but it wasn't easy.

Troy was so relieved to see me when I walked back into his room. His family had left maybe an hour earlier, and I instantly felt horrible, but he said he was asleep. I told him about my day, and he mentioned that I had good friends, and I agreed. Troy ended up getting moved to a regular hospital room, but he still had tubes attached to him due to blood and other drainage, so we had to stay until those could come out. We stayed in the hospital through New Year's Eve and Day. I struggled to stay up until midnight, but I got up and was able to give Troy a New Year's kiss even though it wasn't on the lips, it was still filled with so much love. I couldn't believe this was my life. The year 2017 started with fireworks at the happiest place on Earth with me getting engaged and ended with me curled up in an uncomfortable recliner chair in the hospital with my fiancé listening to machines beeping.

# CHAPTER 30:

## *"Count On Me"*

### - Whitney Houston & Cece Winans

It's hard to go from planning our wedding and travel plans to planning chemotherapy and radiation sessions, AGAIN. We knew it was the best option for Troy though. Troy had about a one-to-two-month break after his surgery, but his doctors were so concerned about having any remnants of the cancerous tumor, that he was put back on Cisplatin AND proton therapy. Preparing for a wedding while also taking care of Troy was hard. Trying to figure out logistics, being financially responsible, and who to really invite was a huge stressor for me. I spent most of the planning phase from a chair next to Troy in the hospital. Some of our close family members and friends reached out to help, and it made it easier. I had my moments where I would just sit down and bust out crying because of all the stress of planning a wedding with the cloud of uncertainty that surrounded me, but also the beauty of all the help that we received along the way. I'm not remiss to know that my dad was shining down on us at particular moments. I took it as his approval of this marriage which was so important to me.

I don't want to seem like we did not have a great planning time, but it was stressful, because Troy was still in treatment, then he had a major surgery the recovery more treatment he had to have eight or nine more cisplatin treatments so the day of the wedding he was recovering from the last cisplatin treatment, so he was getting overheated and sick, but he pushed through it. Even before our wedding, he had to have an MRI scan done and was asked if he wanted to know the results before or after our wedding, Troy chose to find out after the wedding and honeymoon so we could focus on the big day. The planning of it was stressful and it took a lot of my energy, because remember I was the sole breadwinner, the cook, the cleaning lady, chauffeur, and a home health nurse with no medical training. I was adding Event Planner Extraordinaire due to Troy's persistence in getting married. Planning my own wedding added more stress on top of the stress and anxiety I was already living with because of cancer, although I tried not to let Troy see me being stressed because remember caregivers can't show weakness! I tried my hardest to fight through my own pain for him because I knew he wanted to get married so badly. I remember asking to postpone the wedding until he got better, and he absolutely refused because he said that the only reason, he was fighting was to see me walk down the aisle, and on August 11, 2018, that's just what I did! That day was our favorite day of our lives; it was a celebration of not only did Troy make it this far but that two had become one. Troy had fought so hard for that day.

I can't even put it into words, how much our wedding day meant to us. I was grateful to have the chance to get married because of everything that we had been going through in the past year. The wedding day showed me how much of a fighter and champion that Troy was, despite all the trauma and anxiety. We made it to that wonderful day. Getting ready with all my bridesmaids and my Mom, I was surrounded by so much love! I even had a first look with my brother, who again looks so much like my Dad. I'll never forget the look on Paul's face, he looked like, Dad, looking at me and he was speechless. And he was finally able to say, "Ashley you look nice and beautiful". I'll always cherish that memory; with Paul looking so much like my Dad. I took it as another reassurance that this was meant to be.

After I got ready, my friend from Bali said, "Hey, we can sneak out the back door right now if you have any reservations". I looked at her and I said, "No, I'm good. I'm ready. This is my forever". When the music started playing, Troy and I asked for Whitney Houston and CeCe Winans song "Count On Me" to play while the bridal party walked out. We had everyone walk out to that song because of them supporting us individually and together during Troy's battle. Our friends and family stood by us, through hell and now they were able to stand by us in this joyous moment. Before I was due to walk out, I heard the song from John Legend's "All of Me" start playing. I could have picked so many songs to walk down the aisle to, but that song resonated so well with us because Troy loved all of me and I loved all of him, despite our circumstances.

When the curtains opened, Paul was standing to the right of me, and I felt more than ready. Even though I knew Paul was a bit nervous, I was so sure of this moment we were going to have together. Due to our non-traditional ways, I walked up the right side of the sanctuary versus the left. Why? Because my father used to sit to the right of the sanctuary, so in a way I got to look at my Dad, even though he wasn't there physically. As I was walking down the aisle, I was smiling and looking at my King standing next to my Pastor. And when I felt unsure of my footing, I would look down even though I couldn't see my feet. When I looked down into my beautiful bouquet, I was able to see a little picture of my Dad and he would remind me to look up. Keep your head up, as he would always tell me. When I looked at Troy, he started crying, and I was trying not to cry because of this beautiful makeup that I had on. I looked at my bridesmaids, some of them were crying. Looking amongst the crowd, I remember seeing so many of my loved ones, friends, and family, standing there. All these people who had stood by our side, whether it was through the loss of my Dad and/or Troy's cancer diagnosis and treatment, they are now here to witness these nuptials. When I got to the very end of the aisle, my Mom stood up with Paul to give me away.

# CHAPTER 31:

## *"Until The End Of Time"*

### - Justin Timberlake ft. Beyoncé

Troy's vows to me went like this... "Ashley, I love you with all my heart, body, and soul. I wouldn't be here without you in my life. You taught me and showed me what true love is. You are the strongest person I know because you never left, never stopped believing, and never stopped being there for me even when it affected your own life and well-being. I am here because of you, and it is because of you why I get to wake up each day to see your face and smile, also to hear your laugh. As long as my heart beats, I will never stop loving you and making you the happiest wife ever. We are survivors! I am not going anywhere, and I can't wait to see you walk down the aisle and make me the happiest man in the world". I'm trying so hard not to ugly cry at this point!

And I had to follow up those sweet words, while choking back tears! "Troy when I look at you, I don't see what the rest of the world sees. I see a strong man, who continually kicks cancer's butt with style and grace. Watching you fight during your battle is such an inspiration to many and you're so full of life! I knew you channeled your favorite wrestlers, the Rock and John Cena during your battle. I can't believe you got me into watching WWE and ready to enter the ring with you! You're forever my hype man! I love how you always allow me the freedom to pursue my passions and dreams, no matter how crazy they seem. You are there to catch me if I fall.

When I began to pray for you more than I pray for myself, I knew I truly was supposed to be with you. Keep fighting and living! You show me grace and unconditional love, even if I don't deserve it. We will continue to tackle anything that comes our way, and no matter what people say I'll always be there. I'm so excited to live this adventure called life and continue to chase our dreams together until the end of time. No matter what we go through in life I know we'll always have each other's backs. Even though my Daddy is not here physically, I feel his spirit among us, and he gives the thumbs up! We may not have the traditional Disney Princess love story, but it's ours and who wants a damsel in distress when you can have a Pam to your Jim, or a Beyoncé to your Jay-Z? I love you more now and I can't wait to continue to see where our love story takes us"!

In that moment, just telling each other in front of all these witnesses, how much we love each other was so special. No matter what we were going to face in the future, we were going to do it together. When the Pastor said, in sickness and in health, Troy and I looked at each other and laughed, because we had already been there and done that! When we were finally announced as Mr. And Mrs. Thompson, Troy had the biggest smile on his face. That was the goal that he had been wanting to capture for so long. There were times that we didn't know if we would even get to this point and I would question God. All the times I've traveled and admired His beauty and gave Him all the glory. But that same God calls my Dad to Heaven and allows the love of my life to be diagnosed with cancer. For the longest I didn't understand why. What am I supposed to learn? What is wrong with me? But at that moment, on August 11, 2018, I chose to be happy.

# CHAPTER 32:

## "Dance With My Father"

-Luther Vandross

Troy and I couldn't wait to get to the reception a.k.a. the party portion of our wedding. We were so ready to celebrate with all our friends and family as Mr. and Mrs. Thompson! It wasn't just a celebration of our love, but it was also a celebration of Troy's triumph as well! Since Troy and I became fast friends over movies, which blossomed into love, we had a movie theater themed wedding. We had a red carpet, dining tables named after our favorite movies, a popcorn and candy treat table, even our cake was in the shape of an Oscar and movie reel with our pictures on it. When we entered our reception space, we literally had a red carpet rolled out and we felt like celebrities at a Hollywood movie premiere, except this was our real lives. We came in dancing to one of our favorite power couples' songs, Beyoncé and Jay-Z's "Upgrade U", Troy and I felt like our own bootleg version of Jay-Z and Beyoncé that day! Had we not been starving; we would've stayed on the dance floor. Jackson's and Thompson's love to eat. The night was filled with love, laughter, food, and dancing. It is a moment in my life that I wish my Dad would have witnessed, especially when it came time for what would have been the father/daughter dance.

I remember when I had my break down while wedding dress shopping and wanting to honor my father's memory in some way. I also wanted to incorporate my Mom and honor her. Paul and I decided to surprise our Mom during what turned into the brother/sister dance. Paul and I walked out to the floor, and Luther Vandross' song, "Dance With My Father" started to play. I saw my Mom start crying, because the song talks about how a young child grew up in a loving home, now his father is gone, but his mother's heart longs for her husband. And all the child wants is one last dance with his father. Just like I wished I could have had one last dance with my father.

I had someone bring my Mom out to the floor to dance with Paul and I for a couple seconds. Then I removed myself from the dance floor, so Paul, who looks so much like my Dad, could dance with my Mom to the rest of the song. They had such a special moment, I'll forever remember that moment as a tribute to my Dad, and the love that he gave to Paul and me. I know one day we'll be able to dance again together, Dad. There were so many great memories from that day in August, but that's just one memory of how magical our wedding day was. Despite all Troy and I have been through, we could still find small ways to incorporate big meaningful people and moments in our lives. It just added to the beauty and the love of the day.

We were so thankful for what we could do in the time given. We danced the night away with our friends and family, and despite how sick Troy felt, he had to show off his dance skills. We couldn't wait to begin our honeymoon in our favorite happy place, Disneyland.

# CHAPTER 33:

## "The Doctor Said"

-Chole Adams

We flew out to Los Angeles, California to visit Disneyland since our love for Disneyworld is evident, we thought we could give this park a visit! When we arrived at the park, we were able to get pins for our shirts that stated, "HAPPILY EVER AFTER!", I was ecstatic! As soon as we saw Sleeping Beauty's castle and the map of the park, we knew that Disneyworld in Florida was much bigger, but we still couldn't wait to explore! We enjoyed our day there and how great the staff make you feel, knowing that you are on your honeymoon! It was the perfect beginning of our honeymoon.

The next day we flew out to Honolulu, Hawaii. This was Troy's first flight that was over 5 hours long, and I was worried about his comfort, but the flight attendants made sure that we were well taken care of! Since we are huge movie buffs, we booked an ATV tour that would take us along different sites where movies were filmed! We got to see where *Jurassic Park, Pearl Harbor, 50 First Dates, and Lost,* (and so many more) were filmed! Troy and I teared up a bit when we saw where Jurassic Park was filmed because of our love for movies, and those in particular! That was one of the best tours that I have ever been on and we had so much fun! Towards the end of our stay in Honolulu, I could tell that Troy was ready to leave the busy city and go to a quieter island which is exactly what we did!

When we landed on Maui, we got a sense of relaxation and romance. We rented a car because we planned on exploring the island on our own. We got to go to a luau on the beach and it was magical. As the sun was setting, the host welcomed all couples to stand up and dance to a special love song. Troy immediately stood up and grabbed my hand so that we could slow dance together. It was amazing to see the sun rays hitting the water at that exact time, as if they were descending into the ocean. I then looked up into Troy's eye and it was just as blue as that water and my heart skipped a beat in that moment because I couldn't believe how blessed we were to get here and be here in that moment.

Two days after the luau, Maui had started shutting down national parks and certain office buildings due to Hurricane Lane approaching. Troy and I went to the grocery store to stock up on water and food just in case we couldn't get on our flight on August 24th. We had never had to deal with a hurricane before, so we weren't sure what to expect but at least we had each other. The hurricane affected the island in different ways, luckily on our side of the island there were only high winds but on the other side there was flooding and fires. We were so blessed to get to leave and when we did! After we landed in San Francisco, California, we heard that our flight was one of the last ones to leave the island before they cancelled all flights coming in and going out! We felt so blessed and happy to know that we had survived a hurricane! We felt undefeated, if only we had known what this situation was a prelude to...

Upon returning home to Ohio, we had to meet with Troy's

doctor for the follow up on his MRI scan results. We heard the normal click clack of her heels approaching our door and saw the doorknob turn. When she entered, I immediately felt anxious and when I saw her expression, I almost threw up. She looked at Troy first and said, "Troy your MRI results showed that the tumor is growing again and we've exhausted all of the chemo drugs and radiation for your type of tumor, I'm so sorry" and then she turned to me and said, "Ashley, I'm so sorry I know you guys just got married, but you may want to call in hospice at this point and they can help you with next steps". I immediately break down and start crying. How could this be? We just got married and returned from paradise a couple days ago, and now you're telling me that I should call hospice for Troy? While I was still in my moment of defeat, all the sudden I heard Troy yell, "HELL NO! I'm not going out like that! I just married the love of my life and I don't want to die!". He begged the doctor to review his case again and come up with any other remedy. She said she would but not to get our hopes up. Within a week she called us back and told us that the tumor board at the hospital had concluded that the mass could either be a tumor OR necrosis (dying tissue), but the only way to see for sure is to open Troy back up.

Like we really had a choice? We got Troy scheduled for another surgery where they had to reopen him at his first incision across the hairline. Of course, I was nervous due to what happened during his first surgery, but we also trusted the doctors and surgeons that would be in the operating room with Troy. When Troy's neurosurgeon came to speak with me and let me know that it was necrosis, but they had to remove a bit more of his skull bone and a portion of his brain this time. I was a bit afraid because I wasn't sure if he would remember me when he woke up, but the neurosurgeon told me to not worry. When I got to go to the recovery room and see Troy, when he opened his eye and smiled at me, I cried happy tears. I knew he would be ok!

Troy was told that he would need to take Cetuximab, which is an immunotherapy drug that is not technically chemotherapy. The doctors wanted to make sure that there were no remnants of tumor floating around. Troy ended up having 18 doses of that immunotherapy before the doctors wanted to have another MRI scan completed. Troy and I had grown accustomed to having these scans, but it never made them any less stressful! Waiting for results was always filled with anxiety but I'm learning to breathe and jump any hurdle when we come to that.

Troy told me that one day, while I was on my world tour, that he went to my Dad's Holiday Inn (gravesite) and asked for his blessing to marry me. Troy said it was like out of a movie, the clouds parted, and the sun shined right on him and he took that as a sign that my Dad approved. Thankfully all the tears, frustration, and fears melted away on that beautiful day on August 11, 2018 when two became one!

# CHAPTER 34:

## "*Always And Forever*"

-Heatwave

I know watching how my parents loved each other had an imprint on me and how I like to receive love, which if you have never read Gary Chapman's "*Five Love Languages*" book, I HIGHLY suggest it! I realized after reading the book, that I love to receive gifts and acts of service. I often thought that receiving gifts made me shallow, but it isn't! I watched my Dad shower my Mom with gifts even when it was not her birthday or Christmas. He would get her "just because" gifts and the look on her face, when she would receive these gifts stayed with me all these years. It is amazing how our love maps are imprinted and made at such a young age, and I'm so thankful that I had this awesome set of parents to help my marriage be what it is today. At the beginning of our engagement and into our marriage, Troy and I had to learn each other's love language and how we give and receive love. We are two different creatures, when it comes to love.

Troy loves to hear words of affirmation and touch, I love to receive gifts and acts of service. In the beginning of our relationship, we both were giving each other love in the way that we liked to receive it until we knew that we should be giving love how the other one likes to receive it. For example, I was always doting on and spoiling Troy, which he appreciated but he always told me that it was not necessary. Likewise, he would always tell me that he loved me and always wanted to hug me and hold my hand (I had this thing about PDA, I thought it was corny) and I always thought to myself "why does he always have to be touching me?". That is why I think reading the "*Five Love Languages*" book, is so important for singles AND couples because you realize how you need to be loved and don't accept less than. After Troy and I read it, we switched up how we give each other love. Not to say we get it perfect each time, at least we are more aware! I know our love languages could evolve over time as well, like I noticed throughout Troy's treatment it was nice to hear words of affirmation. When I didn't have complete confidence in myself and my caregiver role, he always reassured me that no one else can do what I do for him. It would rejuvenate me in a sense, to keep pushing and praying for our miracle. In those moments, I KNEW it was extremely important for me to give those words of affirmation and touch him because at times he felt so useless and ugly. I was always there to reassure him, that I wasn't going anywhere, and I was dedicated to him and the fight. For these reasons, I'm very thankful I had the foundation and inspiration that I did with my parents!

When I look back, I believe that my Mom received love by words of affirmation and gifts and my Dad received love by words of affirmation. As I mentioned before, that had a lot to do with how I ended up wanting to receive love. My Dad could be hard on us, but he always wanted us to be better than he ever was. I think all parents should want that for their children. I look back on those life lessons and I'm grateful. The nuggets of wisdom that he left for each of us, encircle us every day and sometimes I can hear him whisper to me and guide me along my path.

When I was in the thick of my caregiving journey, my Mom was my backbone. She stood by me with such force and protection. I couldn't have done with this without her, sometimes you just need your Momma! When I didn't feel like cooking, cleaning, or just needed to cry, she was there! I remember asking her, how she held herself together when she was caring for my dying Grandmother so many years ago. She said that her strength came from God and my Dad. I was too young to remember, but apparently my Dad gave her the space she needed to care for her mother, and he filled in the gap when my mother couldn't do all the motherly things for my brother and I; and I thought that statement was powerful. Even though he had never been a caregiver himself, my Dad understood the pressures that could come with it and was her rock and support. My Mom had to care for her and grieve her dying Mom at the same time and my teenage mind couldn't wrap itself around that situation. I'm so thankful that I grew up in a household where I had an example of a leadership team. It truly was a partnership, where one was weak, the other was strong and vice versa. My Mom would allow me to have my moments but then encourage me to take time for myself (but who has time for that?).

I know it hurt my Mom to see me struggling through my caregiver journey, and she always encouraged me to take time for myself, but I couldn't do it. I always felt guilty when I wanted to take time for myself. My Mom knew how much travel revitalized and rejuvenated me, so she mentioned that maybe I should go away before I lost myself. I wasn't too sure, but I ended up going to Chile with one of my best friends and it was a band aid on top of the hurt I felt in that moment. It was refreshing to see different landscapes and see God's beauty and creation, but it also made me think that a God who created such beauty, has allowed my Dad to pass away AND allow my fiancé to battle a rare cancer. How can this be? My Mom encouraged me each day I was gone, and told me that Troy was doing well, I know she could hear the sadness in my voice, and she would pray with me on the phone. I'll always thank God for having her in my life and for being the powerful force in my life, that lets me be me and encourages me to be the best me! My Mom often tells me that my Dad would be so proud of me and especially how I act as a wife, which makes me proud. Even though I'm a grown woman, I still like hearing good remarks from my mother, and I don't think that will ever change.

My Dad is my hero, my best friend and the first man I ever loved! Labor Day of 2011 will always be in my mind, as the day that I lost my Dad and gained a guardian angel. I don't think I will ever understand why HE had to go, he missed out on so many of my big life moments and when I think about my Mom...my heartaches for HER. I remember holding her and consoling her for months afterwards, because you know people stop coming around and checking on you after a couple weeks.

The kind of strength that my Mom exuded, was nothing short of amazing. She often told me that she wasn't sure what she was doing, and she wished that my Dad was here. For me, I thought my Mom handled it well as she could! I poured myself into my Mom and brother, because I have such a protector spirit (I'm so much like my Dad). I didn't really think about my own grieving process, until I was sure that my Mom had started hers. Unfortunately, by that time, I wasn't sure HOW to grieve or if I was strong enough to confront those emotions and feelings.

I know my Dad would have wanted me to be strong and not cry in fear or sorrow, so I didn't for the longest. It wasn't until my Mom told me that it was "ok" for me to start my process, that I did! I knew how I needed to do it too! That is when I quit my job and traveled to about 20 countries, four continents, and countless cities; from Fiji to New Zealand to Vietnam, to Egypt, and then to Albania and Greece, just to name a few!

My Dad wasn't there to walk me down the aisle to Troy, but my brother was! My brother, Paul, is a spitting image of my Dad, and I couldn't have asked anyone else to do the honor of walking me down to the man that I would call my husband.

I recently asked my mother what she thought makes up a strong marriage and she said three things: "Your Dad was always my supporter, protector, and best friend". What a great foundation for a marriage! I always thought it was a great idea to be friends before jumping into anything more serious, and she confirmed that for me. I'm so glad that Troy and I had the foundation of friendship because I needed that to carry me through my own caregiving journey. When that journey got tough, our foundation, along with other support, got me through the darkest times. I'm so proud and appreciative of the example of marriage that I had growing up, and as I pave my way through my own marriage, I continue to use their wisdom and memories to guide me. I know I won't be the perfect wife but knowing that I am Troy's version of a perfect wife, is perfect enough for me!

# CHAPTER 35:

##  "*Your Joy*"

-Chrisette Michelle

❦

Hey Dad! It's Ashley, you're one and only daughter. I must admit...I've been lost without you. You were my best friend and confidant. You would give me sound advice, sometimes I would follow it and other times I wouldn't, but I was young and naïve, can you blame me? That day that Officer Lee and Pastor Hamilton came to our door and told us that you were gone, I literally was in shock and numb by the news. You were so young and so fit; how could this be? Why God? Why MY Dad? We didn't get to do all the things I wanted to; you didn't get to walk me down the aisle to the love of my life. You weren't here when he was diagnosed with a devastating disease, you would've been one of his top cheerleaders because that is what you did! You were a true "ride or die" for your loved ones!

I aspired to be like you so much and over the course of the past 10 years, I feel like I failed many times. One thing about me is that for every time I fail, I would get back up! You and Momma J did not raise a quitter! You both raised a dream chaser and a fighter! Dad, I will always carry your favorite saying in my heart, "You can either have buttprints in the couch or footprints in the sand!". I am your legacy and I feel more at peace with that fact.

I remembered all our talks about how a man should treat me and how I should listen to my intuition. I was listening during those car rides; you always had my attention. Even though I stumbled along the way, I finally found that man who treats me like you taught me to be treated! I'm sad that you didn't get to meet him, because sometimes he does and says things that remind me of you, but I know you are smiling down on us! We see reminders of your love all around us and we are grateful!

I am so glad that I had a great example of marriage to look up to. Daddy, you would love him, although I think you already know him, and you see how Troy makes me smile. No marriage is perfect, but you and Momma J gave me the principles on which we can build a beautiful marriage, and I will show you that I was listening to you, even if it didn't look like it.

Through all this pain with you leaving this Earth and almost losing Troy to cancer, it made me realize my purpose. I'm still amazed that I found my purpose despite my pain and finding this purpose has brought me peace. Daddy, I still miss you every day, but now I can advocate for self-care and help other caregivers celebrate their wins in life. I know you never intended to hurt me, but it was your time. Your time to be celebrated by our Heavenly Father for everything you did on Earth, it was your ultimate gift for your good works and love you shared. Although, I still don't understand death, I understand that I can treasure the moments I have here with my loved ones and that's what I plan on doing for the rest of my days.

Thank you for being the powerful force in my life, wiping my tears, and challenging me to always think and be better. You are part of the reason why I am the woman who I am today. It was truly an honor and reward to call you my Dad for 25 years. I will continue to carry your legacy, while building my own!

Love you forever AND always,
Ashley

# CHAPTER 36:

## "Weathered"

-Creed

Grief can work a number on you, both physically and mentally. It doesn't always look like someone sitting in a dark room crying and being depressed. It can look like someone who is smiling, hardworking, but is extremely exhausted at the end of the day after having to hide their true selves. I hid my hurt and pain with smiling and laughter, my coping mechanism could have been worse, but it still wasn't healthy. I know a lot of you view me as being a strong woman, but I had a lot of self-doubt and lack of confidence during the time after my Dad's passing. I didn't know how to get off the roller coaster of emotions. I was looking for a way out of my own mind. Add being a caregiver on top of still working through grief, and it can compound feelings of anxiety and burnout.

The caregiver cannot show fear! That worked for me for the most part, but that was fake and not healthy!

I know I'm not the only one that has felt lonely! Even if it hurts to be honest with myself...you've felt lonely during this process. You may even have an awesome support system, but do any of them REALLY know how you feel? Probably not. My support system was and still is amazing, but during those times when I found myself alone...I truly felt alone. You know what I mean! It is that time when you leave the doctor's office or during a major surgery when you go within yourself and cry out. You don't let the person you are caring for see because you don't want them to be scared by your reaction to their circumstance.

The fear grips you, almost choking you! My husband, Troy, was diagnosed with a rare nasal cavity cancer in stage 4! I was speechless and Troy was blown away, he immediately started crying. Not one to show fear, I said "we're going to fight". That made him perk up and decide that he wanted to fight the cancer beast!

On the inside, I was crumbling but I didn't dare let him see that! We had JUST gotten engaged about two months prior to his diagnosis, why was this happening to US? The fear of losing someone I wanted to spend the rest of my life with was overwhelming and exhausting, because who knew how much time we had together? For those that know me, I know I may seem like a strong woman, but everyone has a limit! I felt and feared that I was about to reach mine.

I would cry in the shower, curl up in my Mom's arms and just cry until I couldn't anymore. I also sought out different religious and cancer support groups, but what really got me through some of the worst times was good old laughter! Call me crazy, but I laughed off a bunch of my pain and worry. I like the saying, "You have to keep laughing from crying", because most of the time that is what I had as a coping mechanism. I'd rather spend my time smiling and laughing through my circumstance, than crying all the time. How depressing would I become and how would that help Troy's treatment process?

I often questioned God often during the past three years, I would often ask "Why?" and wonder "What am I supposed to be learning from this?". I know the saying "what doesn't kill you makes you stronger", but I was over it. Tired and frustrated with the cancer and treatment that invaded and ravaged my husband's body. I just needed and wanted a miracle, before I totally lost my mind...

What would have been healthy and more helpful is getting therapy at the beginning of his treatment. Glad to be getting help now but should have all along. His remission status even brings some type of loneliness because people stop checking in. All is well because the fight is over, right? Well remission from a cancer brings a new type of fight, one that I'm sure the doctors tried telling us about, but we were so caught up in wanting him to live we might not have listened.

I really wish I would've sought out therapy way before now. Not sure if it would've changed the course of my life, but it would've helped me cope with grief and the responsibilities and anxiety that come with death and caregiving. One of my favorite songs from the band Creed, called *Weathered* explains what anxiety and wanting to crawl out of your own skin feels like!

I never wanted to accept the life that had become mine, even though I knew the reality of my Dad's death and the fact that I was planning a wedding with someone who may die as well. I always felt like the same wound kept getting reopened again and again! Oftentimes, I wish I would've had the tools that I have now to work through my anxiety. Seeking therapy should not be vilified or looked down upon, because it is so helpful and necessary. You can even "shop around" for a therapist that matches you and what type of help you are seeking.

One of my issues was finding the time to seek out therapy and making steady appointments. But you will make time for the things that are important to you, so I finally did that! It is great to have someone to talk to that will be objective and constructive. You can receive unbiased opinions and tools on how to better yourself and situation, which are tools that I wish I would've had way before now. Keeping all the stress and anxiety inside of you is not good and it can make you feel like you're going to implode from within. I do want to add that anxiety and stress can present itself differently to each person. For me, sometimes my heart would race, I would have migraines, ulcers, and would stop eating regularly which caused weight gain. Anxiety can look like wanting to be alone and unbothered, even though you must take care of someone else's needs 24/7. Knowing that all of you, must take care of all of someone else. All the anxiety and stress caused me to burnout. Caregiver burnout is the real deal. We are doing this out of love and compassion, there is no paycheck and little to no help. The world doesn't see what caregivers go through, or even minimizes it, so we tend to keep all our feelings locked up in a box in our mind and heart. I'm letting you know that you can open that box and be free! It may seem hard at first, but once you start talking about your journey and how it has and still is making you feel, you will realize that you are not alone! Despite all that I have been through with my Dad's sudden death and Troy's cancer diagnosis and treatment, I am grateful for the strength I have found to keep pushing and walking in my purpose. One of my friends told me this and I have never forgotten it: Persist Until Something Happens. I encourage you to do the same!

I know some caregivers go through their journeys without acknowledgement from who they care for, so let me give you praise! Take the baby steps to self-care, which can look like seeking out therapy. Mental health is so important! It can cause breakdown of your physical body if it is not taken care of, trust me...I learned the hard way! There is so much emphasis on physically taking care of yourself, like dieting and working out than you mentally taking care of yourself. A healthy well-being is so much more than just the physical aspect. I also believe that when you have started showing love and attention to your own mental state, that you will become a better person for the significant people in your lives. If I didn't start fully working on me, there was no way that I was going to be the best caregiver for Troy! And NOBODY can take care of Troy, like I can!

# CHAPTER 37:

## "The Champion"

-Carrie Underwood ft. Ludacris

In March 2020 Troy was pronounced cancer free and we were so overjoyed. After battling for almost three years, we finally got the miracle that we had prayed for so long. Even Troy's doctors were so happy with the results and his will to keep fighting! The most High was showing off with Troy's victory and we are so grateful! We are so overjoyed and thankful that we have been given another lease on life! We plan to live life to the fullest each day!

Now don't get me wrong, I am ecstatic that we finally got our miracle that we had prayed for and believed for so long! I'm sure along the way of Troy's treatment, all those papers that the doctors gave us and all the warnings they gave us about certain treatments were described but when you are amid a life-or-death situation...you are not thinking of what the side effects can or will be. Specifically in Troy's case due to all the chemotherapy, radiation, and surgeries he has received, parts of his anatomy and day to day living has changed significantly and forever. As I have mentioned before, chemotherapy really makes you sick. In fact, some chemotherapies make you so sick, you may get cancer from the chemotherapy itself!

I remember talking with another wife who happened to be staying in the Hope Lodge with her husband who was fighting cancer throughout his whole body, and she was saying that this was his second fight with cancer. She told me that he had already beaten one type of cancer but was warned that one of his chemotherapy drugs may make the cancer come back and she didn't pay much attention to it, until it DID come back. While she was telling me their story, she had such sadness in her eyes. I mean the cancer came back with a vengeance on his body, it was all throughout but he wanted to fight it! Her last words to me, came to me in a warning but loving tone, please read the side effects of all your fiancé's drugs they give him, be his advocate, and most importantly pray fervently every day for his fight and the unforeseen recovery after that fight. I wish I would've gotten that woman's name, so that I could message her and tell her Troy is cancer free! God gave us our miracle! Maybe she was one of the angels that God sent my way, to comfort and console me in that moment. When I took a harder look at paperwork, I did notice that one of the chemotherapy drugs (cisplatin) has a side effect of cancer. You know how bad my anxiety went up in that moment? Troy had had MULTIPLE rounds of that drug. Obviously, there was nothing that I could do or say because we needed this chemo to kill the cancer cells! Modern medicine uses poison to kill poison in one's body, it's scary and damaging. No one's body is the same after going through chemo and/or radiation. Throughout this entire experience and journey, our lives and bodies have changed but we are stronger together than ever before!

# CHAPTER 38:

## "Love You More"

-Ginuwine

There are times that I feel like a helicopter parent, but for my husband because of certain situations, like his lack of vision. There are times when he can't articulate what he needs, so I speak on his behalf. I've been learning to give him that grace and time for his thoughts to process so that he can articulate his needs for himself, because he's capable of doing it. Because we've been so intimately intertwined for the past three years, I can easily speak for him. I can take one look at Troy, and instantly get a feeling for what is going on with him. I'm learning to give him his own space so that he can navigate his life post cancer. Being in flight or fight mode for so long has our adrenaline in gear and relearning how to become a "normal" couple is hard, so we have decided to become our new normal. When we each need our own space, that's fine! We are individuals that have become one unit, but Troy has his own passions that he wants to pursue, just like I have my own as well.

I know you shouldn't compare yourself to others, but I know Troy and I will always have a different relationship, one that might not always be carefree. We believe and hope that cancer won't come back, but the possibility that it might is real. There are things that I wanted for Troy and me, but he will never be able to do them because physically he cannot! The reality of having to change so many things in our lives because of the devastation that cancer caused is striking. The way we travel, what we do during those travels, and his energy levels get depleted quicker. We used to be avid runners, but I don't know if he'll ever be able to do another half marathon with me. I am not saying these things to complain, I'm telling you the truth and reality of how the nasty cancer beast can wreak havoc. Cancer has stolen some things from me, and US! Watching as some of my friends with their significant others doing the things that maybe I wanted to, but I know we won't get to do those things. It is no one's fault at all, clearly, we didn't ask for this disease.

Cancer doesn't just change the person who was diagnosed, but it changes the person who steps up to be the caregiver too. For me, I know I became stronger, even though I burnt out along the way, I found my voice! You must advocate for your person, because oftentimes they cannot find their own voice. I know he gets frustrated with going to all the doctors' visits and MRI scans, but this is something that we will have to deal with for the rest of our lives. I remind him that it is all to keep him waking up each morning, so that we can love each other and truly live.

I do believe that this whole process has made me love Troy more each day. Despite our situation, I will look at him in amazement at his willingness to fight and be courageous. It has been hard and there were times that I asked him if he felt like I was providing the proper care for him. There were times where I didn't think I was a good caregiver, I would forget things, like medicine, and timing of doctor's visits. I would beat myself up because I didn't think I was the perfect caregiver. I remember I jokingly asked him if he wanted a new caregiver. Troy said, "No, you're the only one that's going to be able to get me through this and keep me alive".

Whenever I would doubt myself, I would remember what he told me. I know I am the best caregiver for Troy, but it was nice to hear it from him. It would give me the confidence I would need to face each day. Even to this day when Troy tells me that it was God and myself that got him through the past few years, my heart soars. I would do anything for Troy, even if the odds are against us. One day I told Troy that I loved him so much, and he responded, "I will love you until the day that I die, plus some".

# CHAPTER 39:

## "Girl On Fire"

### -Alicia Keys ft. Nicki Minaj

I remember calling one of my oldest friends, about Dad passing. I remember she got so quiet, and told me to stop playing, because she had just seen my Dad about a week or two before. In high school, we were always at each other's houses, her Dad became like my second dad, and my parents were like her second parents so I could hear the hurt in her voice. Even though I still wasn't showing much emotion that brought a tear to my eye because of just how much my parents' love meant to her. I'll never forget how quickly she was over to my house to console me and my Mom. I'll never be able to put into words how much I appreciate her, and the support that she gave me in that moment on that day. Our sisterhood and support kept growing through the years. When Troy was diagnosed, she didn't necessarily have words to say but she told me that it was okay to take my time and do what I needed to do for Troy and I.

She told me "You know more than anybody else, that life is not fair. This is the life we are given, and we must walk it out and see where it takes us". And she was so right.

For the longest I didn't understand why life felt so unfair and upsetting. My dad was taken away from me so early, I only had him for 25 years, then at age 30 I had to become a caregiver to the love of my life. In this process called life, I have learned that sometimes your pain brings you to your purpose. Even though we might not like it, we might not like the pathway or journey. But the journey is so necessary and needed to get us to our purpose, and then to share that purpose with the world. That is my mission, I want to share my purpose with the world. Share my purpose driven business with the world and to continue to advocate for caregivers, because you are not alone. I want to advocate for those people that grieve, not only for an actual physical loss, but a loss of a life that you thought you were supposed to have, or thought you were going to have. I celebrate you; I acknowledge you. I hear you, and I see you, and I will continue to advocate for you and with you...to my last breath.

Even though this was what we had prayed for so long, in April, I found myself wondering what I was supposed to be doing with my life at this point. My life for the past three years had been consumed with taking Troy to his doctor's appointments, to treatment, and all the surgeries, so my identity was wrapped up into his care. And now that I wasn't going to have to help him daily, I didn't know what Ashley was supposed to do at this point. I didn't even know what Ashley liked or what Ashley wanted to do with her life at this point, because it had been all about Troy. I oftentimes would start crying because of the fact of not knowing what I was supposed to be doing. I thought I knew what my purpose was, especially after my big "World Purpose Tour" a couple years prior. One day in April 2020, I decided to stop crying and DO something about it.

I invested in myself and I got a business coach. I dove in with both feet, no questions asked because I knew I needed the guidance. Trying to figure out my purpose was my main concern and going through her program and trying to figure that out was important. She asked me to make a list of my likes and dislikes, and the passions that I have in life. not knowing exactly why she was asking me all these questions. I was a little frustrated in the beginning because I just want to know what my purpose is, can't she just tell me or show me? But that's not how finding your purpose works. These types of things take time, I distinctly remember one exercise where we had to talk about Pain versus Pleasure Islands. Obviously, I was currently residing on Pain Island. I had boxed in most of the emotions and anxiety surrounding the sudden death of my Dad, three years of being a caregiver, and not thinking of myself. I had let myself go, all the anxiety that comes with being a caregiver, had caused so much physical pain. So how do I get over to that Pleasure Island? How can I change my circumstances to go across the sea?

As my business coach and I talked more and more, my passion for event planning and travel kept popping up, just as much as my painful parts of my life. During one of our sessions, I had an epiphany! What if I used the pain points in my life to plan events and/or travel for the terminally and chronically ill and their loved ones!?! I know the pressures that caregivers go through and what grief feels like. As you know, I planned my wedding not knowing if I was going to be able to marry that person that I was planning it with. I can use my own personal pain and turn it into my purpose.

With that epiphany, Timeless Dream Events was born, which is an event company that plans weddings, birthdays, and/or a celebration of life, for those that are terminally or chronically ill, and their loved ones. What makes Timeless Dream Events different is the fact that we can plan whatever you need within a short time frame. We understand the unique and specific needs that come with time and financial constraints, and I am more than willing to help! We will make this an incredibly special event and take into consideration the sensitivity of your situation. We will make a "Timeless Dream Event" for you that will last a lifetime, because cherished memories are everlasting! Being that light and love that people need in that time of life, I'll be there. I know what it feels like to be planning a big event in life and not knowing if that person is going to make it. Knowing what my purpose in life is, makes me wake up with a grateful heart and excited to start the day. I appreciate the outpouring of love and support for my family and I over the years. I'm so excited to start this new chapter of life and see where it takes us! I hope you enjoyed this part of my journey and thank you for allowing me to be vulnerable, my heart is soaring high in a way that I haven't felt in the past. Remember to always chase your dreams, have integrity, and aim high! Be well and be blessed! I know now that my Dad is still pushing me to be the best version of myself, even from Heaven! Knowing that I may be able to help, even just one person sets my soul on fire!

I am dedicated to helping caregivers along their journey! It can be painful, you can suffer great loss, but take it from a Phoenix rising, that you can see a glimmer of hope. Have you ever heard of the mythological creature called a "Phoenix"? Well, a Phoenix is known to be this huge, majestic bird that lives for hundreds of years before bursting into flames. What's so awesome about the Phoenix, is that it is born out of the ashes to start a new life! I tell you about the Phoenix because I feel like the Phoenix, in that I am rising out of the ashes into something new and grand! You're allowed to be able to treat yourself, you can love yourself, and let someone like me be able to help you through your time of pain and heartbreak by celebrating life and love! That is the purpose and mission behind Timeless Dream Events.

I am genuinely excited for the people I have met along this journey, and the people that I will continue to meet. Having a purpose driven business, fulfills those thoughts of lack and despair. Knowing that I can make an impact, is all that I could want in this lifetime and what my parents prayed for. I don't have to rely on other people's outreach for my own sanity or sense of belonging. Constantly staying prayed up and staying as positive as possible, is how I choose to live my life and go into any battle that may come my way in the future. My story is still being written.

# CHAPTER 40:

## "*Superstar*"

-Usher

On the day that my Dad passed, he told my Mom "There are some things that you are going to have to figure out on your own." She told me that it was in response to her asking a question and that it has taken almost 10 years since his passing to understand what he meant. Like myself, my Mom had questioned why my Dad passed away so early. She mentioned that "These last 10 years has been filled with challenges, fear, love, and triumph, so many different emotions, but mostly learning who I am through my grieving journey and what he taught me. Your Dad believed in me when I didn't even believe in me!". I found this statement very profound, because I often felt the same way about Troy during my caregiver journey. I always felt like I was failing him and not good enough, I would often tease him and mention "Maybe you should hire a new caregiver because I'm slacking." Troy would always respond with, "No. No one else would ever replace you and I'm still alive because of YOU!". I'm supposed to be taking care of him and he is encouraging me and speaking strength into my soul! Those encouraging words kept driving me forward and kept me pushing on! Troy depended upon me too, he was not ready to die so we put up a fight...TOGETHER! Even with the launch of my new business, Troy was right behind me 110% and encouraging me. Troy nurtures me when I'm feeling weak, gives me space when needed, and was and is my forever fan!

Troy truly makes me feel like a superstar when I don't feel like it that day. He constantly reminds me that there are great men in this world and I'm so grateful that I found one for myself, like my Dad prayed that I would. I will always advocate and fight for you Troy, you have weathered the storm and come out with a smile on your face. What a titan and champion that even Hercules couldn't defeat.

# CHAPTER 41:

## "You'll Be In My Heart"

-Phil Collins

A s life will have it, I was never fully able to put my caregiving hat up. My Grandpa has been diagnosed with terminal cancer, so I help my Mom care for him. This time is different because I use the tools that I have figured out along the way during my caregiver journey with Troy. Being the best caregiver that I possibly can be, respecting my boundaries, providing my own self-care, and making sure my Mom is exercising the proper self- care for herself. Burnout is all too real, and it can happen very easily and fast. Knowing what triggers your stress and anxiety can help you combat the severity of it. I know it's hard to get completely rid of stress and anxiety as caregivers, but I can navigate around "Burnout City." I don't have to go there; I can steer away in the other direction from it.

You're going to have your good days, and you're going to have your bad days. But as long as you remember that taking care of your body so that you can help somebody else is especially important. Taking the lessons that I've learned throughout my caregiver journey with Troy, I implement them into taking care of my grandfather and any other future caregiving needs that may arise.

I don't believe I will ever hang up my caregiver hat; it's just not me. But like I said before, I don't ever have to lose myself in being a caregiver; I don't have to ever lose my identity again. I have learned to love myself more. Loving yourself is not selfish; it shows strength. It shows that you care, not only for yourself but the person that you're caring for! Because like I mentioned before, if my body breaks down, if I'm not taking care of myself mentally, physically, or spiritually, then who's going to take care of Troy, who's going to take care of my grandfather, or anybody else in the future that I may have to take care of? Who's going to do it the best? I know I am the best for the situation that may arise. So, Ashley must take care of Ashley, and I highly encourage you to do the same. Seek out therapy. Pick up a new hobby, whether it's coloring, journaling, walking, running, reading a book, listening to music, cooking, or binge-watching a Netflix series. Whatever it looks like for you, just try it with baby steps. Don't allow yourself to get so stressed out that you make yourself sick. If I haven't shown you enough, it has detrimental effects on you mentally and physically. You might not feel like you're living your best life, and that's okay. But what is not okay is keeping all those feelings of stress and anxiety bottled up because one day, it will explode. Self-care equals self-love, and you should love yourself. You're doing great work, and you should recognize that for yourself. You are loved, and you are appreciated. You are an amazing caregiver. You're an amazing person. Remember that. Always.

# CHAPTER 42:

## "When You Wish Upon A Star"

-Cliff Edwards

Going to Disney was and is always a special treat for me. We had the pleasure to go as a family recently, and we wanted to reenact our time with Dad from almost 25 years ago. We knew it wouldn't be the same, but it was so special and surreal for my Mom, Paul, and I to be together, almost 25 years later at Disneyworld. We laughed and reminisced about the times that we had had with Dad. We took pleasure in knowing that we had a good life with him even though it was short. Even though he couldn't physically be with us on this trip, we had the best time, and we realized that we were able to keep his playful spirit alive. My mom was apprehensive about riding some of the rides this time around, but she did it! The ride called Space Mountain will forever be remembered as an infamous ride to our family because it was Paul's first roller coaster, and it scared him senseless. The first time we went to Disney, I was 10, and Paul was 4 years old, so it probably wasn't smart for him to be on this ride, but we didn't know that it was going to be as fast and quick as it was! I remember my dad holding him in the seat, and as soon as it took off, we knew it was going to be bad. When we got off that ride, my four-year-old brother kicked my dad in the shin because he was so scared. I know my Dad had to have felt bad for allowing Paul to ride that roller coaster! My Dad was such a protector, and even though as we got older, we could laugh about that situation, I'm sure there was a moment where my Dad felt like he had let Paul down.

We rode Space Mountain like CHAMPS. After we got off, we all just laughed at how four- year-old Paul had gotten so mad at dad for taking him on that ride, and now we enjoyed it. It was just a special time for us to bond, as adults, and reconnect with each other, love each other. The three of us were able to not only talk about the past but also talk about our present and future and what it might look like.

My Mom, Paul, and I want to find what brings us joy in life and pursue that; no matter what your age is or your circumstances, finding that peace of joy that you can insert into your life is so important. Of course, being at the happiest place on earth (to me), I was just constantly reminded again of how much Disney means to me and my life. It was the first airplane ride I got to take at 10 years old with my family, and throughout the years, being able to take Troy for his first time, taking my stepdaughter, Koby, for the first time. On January 1st, 2017, getting the most amazing proposal that any woman could have asked for in front of Cinderella's castle, then starting my honeymoon at Disneyland. Now finally, 25 years later from the first time that I had ever been going with my Mom and my brother for my 35th birthday.

It's been a great ride. It's been amazing to celebrate some of life's biggest changes and biggest milestones at Disney and surrounded by loved ones. I do believe, no matter what happens in life, Disney will always be my happy place. It will always remind me of my Dad and a reminder that magic truly exists. It doesn't matter what age or how many times I've been; I will always have a love for Disney and what it means to me. Even though the park changes over time, the special feeling of the magic of Disney will never dim for me. All you must do is "wish upon a star" like Jiminy Cricket sang in Pinocchio.

Sometimes a hope and a wish are all you have, and I am ok with clinging onto hope. I hope that cancer doesn't strike again in a devastating way, hope that I can grow old with Troy, hope that I can fulfill my heart's desires. Hope and belief are so powerful, and they are a beacon to guide my path, a path that God has truly lit up for me in my darkest hours.

# References

Alicia Keys feat. Nicki Minaj. "Girl On Fire." RCA Records, 2012.

Alicia Keys. "Superwoman." Sony Music Entertainment, 2007.

Amerie. "Why Don't We Fall In Love." Sony Music Entertainment, Inc., 2002.

Beyoncé. "Upgrade U." Sony BMG Music Entertainment, 2006, 2007.

Bill Withers. "Lean On Me." Sony Music Entertainment, 1994.

Blue Ivy, SAINt JHN, Beyoncé & Wizkid. "Parkwood Entertainment LLC." *Brown Skin Girl*. Columbia Records, 2020.

Bob Marley & The Wailers. "One Love/People Get Ready." The Island Def Jam Music Group, 2002.

Caitlin & Will. "Address In The Stars." Sony Music Entertainment, 2009.

Carrie Underwood feat. Ludacris. "The Champion." UMG Recordings, Inc., 2018.

Chic. "Good Times." Atlantic Recording Corporation, 1991.

Chloe Adams. "The Doctor Said." Chloe Adams, 2017.

Chrisette Michele. "Your Joy." The Island Def Jam Music Group, 2007.

Cliff Edwards & Disney Studio Chorus. "When You Wish Upon A Star." Walt Disney Records, 2001.

Creed. "Weathered." Wind-Up Records, LLC, 2004.

Diana Ross & Lionel Richie. "A Motown Records Release." *Endless Love.* UMG Recordings, Inc, 1981.

DMX. "Party Up." The Island Def Jam Music Group, 2010.

Faith Evans. "Soon As I Get Home." Bad Boy Records, 1995.

Ginuwine. "Love You More." Sony Music Entertainment Inc., 2002, 2003.

Heatwave. "Always And Forever." GTO Records LTD., Sony Music Entertainment Inc., 1977, 1978, 1979, 1980, 1982.

Janet Jackson. "Miss You Much." A&M Records, 2009.

Janet Jackson. "Runaway." A&M Records, 2009.

John Legend. "All Of Me." Getting Out Our Dreams and Columbia Records, 2013.

Journey. "Don't Stop Believin'." Sony Music Entertainment, 1988.

Justin Timberlake feat. Beyoncé. "Until The End Of Time." Zomba Recording LLC, 2006.

Kirk Franklin. "Looking For You." Zomba Gospel LLC, 2005.

Lecrae. "Fear." Reach Records, 2014.

Luther Vandross. "Dance With My Father." Sony Music Entertainment, 2003.

Mariah Carey. "Hero." Sony Music Entertainment, 2001.

Mary Mary. "Can't Give Up Now." Sony BMG Music Entertainment, 1999, 2000.

Mary Mary. "It Will All Be Worth It." Sony BMG Music Entertainment, 2008.

Michael Jackson. "Remember The Time." MJJ Productions Inc., 1979, 1982, 1987, 1991, 1995, 2001, 2005.

Michael Jackson & Janet Jackson. "Scream." MJJ Productions Inc., 1979, 1982, 1987, 1988, 1991, 1995.

Michael Jackson. "Thriller." MJJ Productions Inc., 1982.

Natalie Cole. "This Will Be (An Everlasting Love)." Capitol Records, Inc., 1975.

New Edition. "Can You Stand The Rain." UMG Recordings, Inc., 1988.

Peter, Paul, & Mary. "Leaving On A Jet Plane." Warner Records Inc. Manufactured & Marketed by Rhino Entertainment Co., 2005.

Phil Collins. "You'll Be In My Heart." Edgar Rice Burroughs, Inc. and Walt Disney Records, 1999.

Sister Sledge. "He's The Greatest Dancer." Atlantic Recording Corporation and Brookhill Records Corporation, 1995.

Survivor. "Eye Of The Tiger." Volcano Entertainment, III, L.L.C., 1991.

Tauren Wells. "God's Not Done With You." Provident Label Group LLC, a division of Sony Music Entertainment, 2017.

The Weeknd. "Can't Feel My Face." The Weeknd XO, Inc., marketed by Republic Records, a division of UMG Recordings, Inc., 2021.

Usher. "Superstar." LaFace Records, 2004.

Whitney Houston & CeCe Winans. "Count On Me." Arista Records LLC, 1995.

Whitney Houston & Mariah Carey. "When You Believe." Arista Records LLC, 1998.

50 Cent. "In Da Club." Shady Records/Aftermath Records/Interscope Records, 2003.

# *Resources*

Timeless Dream Events: Ashley Jackson
www.timelessdreamevents.com

Caring for the Caregiver Facebook group:
https://www.facebook.com/groups/caregiverstreatyoself

Caregiver Coach: Meriam Boldewijn
https://meriamboldewijn.com/

Dementia Caregiver Wellness: Marina Rieboldt-O'Neill
http://www.cognitivevitality.net/

Millennial Caregiver resources:
www.i-ally.com

Grief Connection resources:
www.mygriefconnection.org

Trauma & Emotional Healing Counseling: Gunjani Patel,
MA, NCC, LPCC, LMHC, CISM, ABA
www.gpatelcounseling.com

Business Coach: Sonjia "Lioness" Mackey
https://www.facebook.com/groups/MediocrityEscapologists/

Editor/Writing Coach: Dr. Sarah Jefferis
www.sarahjefferis.com

Self-Publishing Help: Jo Cabey
https://www.journeywithjo.com/shop-category/services

Travel Agency: BeHUEmane
www.behuemane.com